A NEW DESIGN FOR HIGH SCHOOL EDUCATION

A NEW DESIGN FOR HIGH SCHOOL EDUCATION

ASSUMING A FLEXIBLE SCHEDULE

Robert N. Bush

Professor of Education
Stanford University

Dwight W. Allen

Assistant Professor of Education
Stanford University

McGraw-Hill Book Company, New York · San Francisco · Toronto · London

A New Design for High School Education

Library of Congress Catalog Card Number: 63-23385

456789 VB 10987

PREFACE

Secondary education in the United States has been an exciting venture since its earliest Latin grammar school days. No period has been without lively ferment even though discussions of change often did not influence the classroom. The transformation of the Latin grammar school to the modern American high school reflects in many ways the developmental history of this country— a constant shaping and invention to meet the emerging conditions of a new way of life dedicated to the high purposes of freedom and opportunity for an entire people.

The ever swifter pace of change that has characterized the modern world has become even more accentuated since the end of World War II. Modern technology impinges upon education with increasing force. It both demands change and makes possible achievements never before dreamed of. The explosion of knowledge renders a new curriculum obsolete almost before it is put into place. Changing occupational patterns require that the training programs in schools achieve a degree of flexibility never before anticipated. Educational demands placed by society upon each young person growing up today and the new possibilities now envisioned for realizing the potential inherent in each person have combined to cause the level of education considered minimum for each young person to leap far ahead of that for the current generation of adults.

These new possibilities and demands have generated pressures that so bear down upon the high school as to cause it to burst apart unless a new design with greater flexibility is introduced to guide its present operation and to permit it to respond and adapt.

The new design reported here, which charts a course for the high school of the future, is a technical rather than a humanistic document. Thus will it disappoint some, for it suffers the general faults of the day. It will bring small comfort to those who are concerned with the pace at which giant computers, automation, teaching machines, mass media, and other mechanizations hurtles us "forward" into a brave new world. Nonetheless, if education is to be moved genuinely forward in these days, a technical approach is necessary. No longer will the philosophical polemics, which have for so long enlivened discussions of educational matters, alone suffice.

If sufficient attention is paid by the reader to the initial part of the report (especially Chapters 1 and 2), he will note the basic plea that *all*—not just a selected part of the oncoming generation—be liberally educated. This is not a technical proposition, nor an argument of recent vintage. Chapter 2, which presents the basic assumptions upon which the proposal rests, goes directly to the heart of the educational question: What should be taught—not to everyone but to each one, and how should we organize our school program to accomplish this? It and the preceding first chapter, which points up the nature of the current education problem, deal with both the ends and the means of high school education, which in our view are inseparably linked and constantly influencing each other. The succeeding chapters, which make up the bulk of the report, deal with implementing the propositions set forth in the beginning and are quite technical and detailed. Thus most of the report may prove to be not exciting or easy to read, but difficult to follow, especially because of the new terminology and concepts necessary to describe what is being proposed.

The modern high school is a large, complex organization. To realize the changes necessary to keep it abreast of the times becomes an urgent, difficult task. We need to be clear not only in what to do, but also on how to implement the changes that are necessary. Educational change today probably hangs up more on the lack of technical competence for implementation than it does on disagreement over what changes should take place. Until recently we have not been technically able to organize a school along sufficiently flexible lines so that the general requirements for all and the individual needs of each pupil can be met. Now, fortunately, long-sought traditional values, together with new goals, can be realized in the high schools of today and tomorrow, without dehumanizing the process, if we but use the technical forces at our command.

This *New Design for High School Education* is offered for discussion because of the need for a new framework within which to consider high school education. The possibilities inherent in the burgeoning of new developments (team teaching, teaching machines, programmed learning, flexible scheduling, and new curricula in the basic disciplines) are unprecedented. One main difficulty in the past has been that the old design was a closed system. The many exciting developments in this decade are only precursors of many more and different ones in the next. Those that now look promising and bright may either not work or soon become obsolete. There is need for a new design that is open but that can be outlined with sufficient precision to be capable of adoption and experimentation in a variety of situations. The new design presented here meets these requirements. It is open in that schools with different educational assumptions and persuasions can cooperatively experiment. It not only permits but encourages experimentation and change.

This technical report is addressed primarily to the teachers and administrators who are concerned with high school education, whether they are in high schools or in colleges and universities. School board members and interested laymen may also find interest in some of the basic educational ideas in the earlier part of the report.

Many have contributed to this report. The Ford Foundation and its Fund for the Advancement of Education have through substantial grants made possible a comprehensive structure of investigation in secondary education at Stanford University over the past five years. In this, the steady leadership of Alvin C. Eurich has been most helpful. In the technological investigations of school schedule construction through the use of electronic computers, the continuing help of Lester W. Nelson and Edward J. Meade, Jr., of the Fund have been indispensable. I. James Quillen, Dean of the School of Education at Stanford University, has provided a favorable environment to conduct the investigations of the Secondary Education Project. His support and encouragement are deeply appreciated. The faculty in secondary education at Stanford have contributed generously in hours and ideas to the development of the framework of the new design. Without exhausting the list, mention must be made particularly of Harold M. Bacon in mathematics, Alfred H. Grommon in English, Richard E. Gross in the social studies, Paul DeH. Hurd in the sciences, June K. McFee in art, Rudolph Morgan and Ruth Weir in foreign languages, Wolfgang Kuhn in music, Helen W. Schrader in speech and drama, Frederick J. McDonald in psychology, and Norman J. Boyan in administration. John Nixon, in addition to helping with general ideas, has developed in detail a comprehensive new framework for high school physical education based upon the framework of the new design. A new design for high school education has become possible because computers can now be used to generate the entire school schedule, thanks to the original work of our colleague Robert V. Oakford of the industrial engineering faculty.

Our students in the doctoral seminar in secondary education at Stanford University over the past few years have made substantial contributions to development of the ideas in the new design. In this group we are especially indebted to Scott D. Thomson, Harry L. Garrison, and James Olivero, who also assisted substantially in the preparation of the manuscript.

None of these or others who contributed so much to what may prove to be strengths of the report can be held accountable for its weaknesses. For these, we alone assume full responsibility.

Robert N. Bush · Dwight W. Allen

CONTENTS

A NEW DESIGN
FOR
HIGH SCHOOL
EDUCATION

1

A FRAMEWORK FOR
HIGH SCHOOL EDUCATION

The idea of secondary education that has developed in the United States has been one of this country's boldest thrusts on the frontier of human affairs. During the eighteenth and nineteenth centuries America forged the new concept that secondary schools should be freely available to all youth who wished to attend. Then in the first half of the twentieth century the United States took another bold step by making education compulsory, not just through elementary school but also through the secondary school years. This revolutionary goal of a high school education for all has been almost achieved, and, until recently, no other country ever envisioned, much less attempted, to realize such a goal. But events race onward as ideas flow quickly and forcefully around the modern world. Following World War I, countries in many parts of the world observed the unprecedented level of material well-being that the United States had achieved. Surmising that this well-being was not unrelated to the extensive provision for schools in the United States, these countries have been adopting for themselves this same goal of compulsory secondary schooling and have been rapidly expanding and democratizing their schools.

A further unique feature of secondary education in the United States, in addition to its universal character, has been the *comprehensive* high school, that high school in each community which serves everyone irrespective of his status or aim in life. Here have mingled the bright and dull, the devout and heathen, and the

1

children of the rich and of the poor. In place of the rigid test systems and systems of separate schools developed in Europe, the United States offers its children the comprehensive high school.

Even though some recent criticisms have suggested that secondary schools in the United States should revert to the European pattern mentioned above, it now appears that this alternative is not acceptable and that the basic idea of a comprehensive secondary school remains sound for this country. But the extensive critical public discussion of the American high school has led to the conclusion that even though the high school was a pacesetter in the last century and has been a vital factor in helping to achieve a high standard of living, this is no time for complacency. Quite the opposite. Now is the time to move in new directions and to dream again a new American dream and conceive a new standard for ourselves and possibly for the world.

The *new* goal which is now beginning to emerge refers not to amount and numbers (i.e., everyone in school for a given number of years)—a quantitative standard of the past—but rather to a *quality* of excellence to be achieved in the education provided for everyone in high school. While the debate over what shall constitute an education of the highest quality for each pupil has not been concluded, more than a suggestion emerges that the new aim may be even more lofty in its conception than its predecessor. The new goal emerging from public discussion of secondary education is this: All youth shall, by the end of compulsory schooling, be so launched in a broad, liberal education that they will continue such education as a lifelong pursuit. Further, each person's education will have been so planned that he will have opportunity to develop, as early as his talents are discovered, and be encouraged to develop one or more lines of specialization which will represent the flowering of his own unique interests and abilities. In the past the plan has been to encourage a liberal education for those going to the university and into the professions and a specialized vocational training for those going immediately to work. In Europe those two educational streams have been diverted to separate schools; in the United States they are both in one school, the comprehensive high school. But the new concept is one that holds that the level of education needed in the next half-century—adequate to meet the needs of the nation as well as of the individual—requires that for everyone both a liberal and a specialized education shall have been well begun by the end of compulsory schooling.

Already overcrowded with pupils, with more to come, and confronted with the necessity for reaching higher levels of excellence than ever before regardless of severe shortages of teachers and finances, the American high school must evolve new, more efficient and effective measures to its ends lest it fail in its new mission. Despite these formidable obstacles, there is reason to be optimistic, for already signs may be seen in secondary schools throughout the country that teachers and administrators are working to turn this crisis into new educational opportunities. For example, national commissions of scholars, teachers, and educationists are at work revising the high school curriculum. Experimentation with television, tape recorders, teaching machines, and other technological aids is opening new vistas for producing and enhancing learning. While each of the many innovations appears promising, they cannot all be fitted into the high school program as it is now organized. Also, administrators concerned with the several subject-matter fields are convinced that they could provide better programs if they had more and better-prepared teachers with lighter pupil loads, if they had more of the pupils for longer periods of time, and if they had greatly expanded and improved facilities. Obviously, all that each group wants cannot be granted; for time, money, staff, and space are limited.

In a concern with trying to organize secondary schools for everyone, the high school[1] has developed a standard system of units and credits, and all subjects meet for the same number of minutes per

---

[1] "High school" as used here refers to grades 7 to 12. This assumption is discussed in Chap. 2.

period and periods per week for pupils of all levels of ability. Everyone, the present regulations commonly state, shall take five years of English before graduating, which means 55-minute daily periods for each of the thirty-six weeks of the two semesters. One chief shortcoming of such standardization has been that with physical education required each year, English for five of the six years, and social sciences for four years, pupils are shortchanged in their education in science, mathematics, foreign languages, and the arts—subject fields of profound and growing importance in these times. With mounting knowledge and increased sophistication about children, their educational needs, and how they learn, it becomes difficult to ignore the fact that not all children do need the same amount of time to learn specific things. Nor do all children come to school with equal backgrounds and talents. Some pupils entering high school are already more advanced in a subject than others will be upon graduation. Some will be able to communicate in a second language after two or three years' study; others will take five or six years to develop this same communication skill. Some pupils with excellent achievement and background in one subject would be better off if they were to spend their time in studying another subject rather than in serving time to meet a requirement. The present lockstep of six years to graduate and rigid set of course requirements makes little sense. Hard and fast rules that will fit all pupils are difficult if at all possible to find. Thus while the curriculum as a whole must be designed, that portion of it in which each individual is scheduled to enroll should result from an objective, highly personalized diagnosis of his needs. Pertinent questions emerge: Could not requirements be arrived at and stated more flexibly so that these important differences in pupils are taken into account? Would not some kinds of subjects better be taught in large blocks of time and others in shorter and more frequent time periods? The answers are obviously yes, but as practical school administrators and teachers ask: How can programs of such flexibility be scheduled?

The promising results of many experiments now in progress will depend for their wide application upon arranging the schedule of the high school so that these different courses and curricula can be accommodated. To make possible the fitting together of separate facets of the problem, a new design for high school education must be formulated. This design should strike a balance between curricular requirements and electives; it should not only guarantee the absence of significant gaps in the education of any pupil but also take adequate account of that pupil's individuality. This new design should provide flexible arrangements for the conducting of classes, arrangements which consider not only the pupils' differences, but consider those unique talents and specialized competences of teachers and differences in the subject fields as well.

The possibility of developing a flexible high school schedule to serve educational needs of pupils has become a reality with the advent of electronic data-processing procedures and high-speed computers. These machines have been used in a variety of complex industrial, governmental, and military applications. They mark a new industrial revolution—freeing men from mental labors more prodigious than the physical labors eliminated by the power revolutions of the past two centuries. As a school schedule becomes more varied to provide for new levels of individualization, the number of schedule alternatives increases geometrically. What is an odious task under current practice becomes an impossible task without mechanical assistance. The magnitude is incredible—if an 80-period week is used for 1,800 students, it would take a computer capable of a million operations a second about twenty-five years to systematically consider all alternatives possible for a single schedule. Prof. Robert V. Oakford of Stanford University indicates that, based on the pioneering work he is directing, the application of these modern procedures to high school scheduling appears most promising. The use of computers, however, demands a much more thorough analysis of the problems and decisions involved than has been necessary under more straightforward manual systems of scheduling. It is important to identify the appropriate contribution of machine technology. It is erroneous ever to assume that machines will be able to *make decisions.* They can only *implement decisions* involving an intricate series of interlocking factors, each of which can be reduced to logical alternatives. Further, the use of computers can suggest new alternatives to consider, based upon more sophisticated procedures uniquely related to machine capability.

The proposals presented in the next chapters are offered in the hope that, as they are further developed and tested, they may help to remove the fetters which now encumber many attempts to experiment in this area. The motto of those building this framework is: Take away the limitations. Those working in each subject-matter field, as well as those who have responsibility relating to the organization and administration of the school enterprise, those who teach there, those charged with interpreting its responsibilities to reflect public policy, and those who prepare its practitioners, are invited to consider these questions: If, in high school, you could provide all pupils with an ideal program of study in each subject, how would you arrange the instruction? What would be your aims? For which different groups of pupils would you provide? Would each group take the same curriculum, but at a slower or faster pace? Or would you have different aims, different materials, and different amounts of time for the teaching of pupils of different abilities and interests? What kind of a staff would you provide? What size classes would be most desirable? What content would be most useful? How would you evaluate the results? These are the challenges. Tentative suggestions of what might be accomplished with this approach are outlined in the next chapters.

2

ASSUMPTIONS ABOUT CURRICULUM STUDY AND FLEXIBLE SCHEDULING

The high school curriculum as well as the schedule by which the curriculum is organized stems from a set of values and specific decisions about instruction, students, and schools. The first step in designing an educational program is to make explicit the assumptions on which the program rests. The proposals outlined here rest upon the following seven assumptions:

1. High school is the period of schooling typically included in grades 7 to 12.

2. All students should have continuous, rigorous study in breadth and depth in all basic subject[1]-matter fields throughout the six secondary school grades. These fields are:

   a. *Arts* (visual, performing, practical).
   b. *Languages* (English and foreign).
   c. *Mathematics.*
   d. *Natural sciences.*
   e. *Physical education and health.*
   f. *Social sciences.*
   g. *Guidance.*[2]

[1] A *subject* is a broad general curriculum area for which the scope and sequence of content are conventionally defined and arranged as *courses*, for example, French, mathematics, English.
[2] See Chap. 7 for clarification of this new concept of guidance.

3. In each subject area several groups of students whose needs are sufficiently distinct to require a discrete program of studies can be identified.

4. Each subject, when properly taught, will include four basic types of instruction:

   a. Independent and individual study.
   b. Small-group instruction.
   c. Laboratory instruction.
   d. Large-group instruction.

5. Adequate instruction in each subject-matter field requires senior teachers who are both well trained in their subject-matter field and highly skilled in teaching and who are assisted by less highly trained members of the instructional and supporting staff.

6. Class size, length of class meeting, and the number and spacing of classes ought to vary according to the nature of the subject, the type of instruction, and the level of ability and interest of pupils.

7. It is possible to obtain scheduling assistance through the use of data-processing equipment in order to implement a large degree of schedule flexibility.

Elaboration of Basic Curriculum Assumptions

1. *High school is the period of schooling typically included in grades 7 to 12.*

In the nineteenth century and during the early years of the twentieth century, the American high school was considered to be a four-year institution consisting of grades 9, 10, 11, and 12. It rested on an eight-year elementary school. The break between elementary and secondary education occurred between grades 8 and 9, when most of the pupils were about thirteen to fourteen years old. Beginning in the second decade of the present century, this structure has been in the process of reorganization. The break between elementary and secondary education has been moved back two years so that it now occurs for a majority of pupils after grade 6, when they are at the age of eleven to twelve years. American education is coming in this particular to be more in line with education elsewhere in the world. Even though this structure has not become a nationwide policy, the trend runs strongly in that direction; consequently, in this discussion secondary education is used to refer to that period typically included in grades 7 through 12, in which pupil age span is from roughly eleven years to seventeen or eighteen years. Thus, the beginning of secondary education occurs for the pupil at about the onset of puberty. At this time schooling begins to be directed by teachers who are specialized in separate disciplines, and pupils are separated into special classes for each subject. High school, then, is viewed as a continuous six-year program.

2. *All students should have continuous, rigorous study in breadth and depth in all basic subject-matter fields throughout the six secondary school grades.*

The second and far-reaching assumption represents a major departure from traditional as well as from much present practice. With the possible exception of English and physical education, traditional practice has not encouraged a continuity of study distributed over the six-year span. Required subjects have in the past been grouped conveniently in those certain years and semesters considered most appropriate for a nonexistent typical student. Segmental isolation of many required and elective courses[1] has resulted, and learning losses due to forgetting and weak articulation of subject sequences have been considerable. Columbus predictably

---

[1] A *course* is a unit of instructional material taught during a specific time period (semester or year); for example, French is a *subject*, but French 2 is a *course*.

sails on schedule in the fifth-, eighth-, and eleventh-grade required courses in American history without any attempt made to build upon previous learning.

This second proposition assumes that most students should continue to build and strengthen, throughout their high school careers, their understandings and competences in the visual, performing, and practical arts,[2] in languages, both English and foreign, in mathematics, in natural science, in physical education and health, and in the social sciences. A minimum sequence for each subject-matter field helps assure a common cultural core for all beyond which each student may elect variations in depth and breadth to fulfill his own unique needs and potentials. This basic continuous fare provides for all the educational nourishment which each must have in an increasingly interdependent society of specialists, for it protects against the unbalanced diet of premature specialization. It seeks to assure that students continue to be broadly educated as they specialize.

All the basic subject-matter fields suggested above are seen to have values which make desirable their inclusion in the high school continuum. For full realization of this desirability, each department of instruction will need to design, at each grade level, courses which articulate with pre-high school and post-high school offerings, which provide sequential development eliminating needless duplication and redundancy, which integrate intelligently with other subject-matter sequences, and which challenge and develop individual potential and talents by appropriate variations in breadth and depth.

There are three types of curricular elements which should be included for all students in each subject area to be studied in the new design. These three general curricular types can be identified

---

[2] Included in this category are industrial arts and homemaking, as well as music, painting, crafts, sculpture, and dramatics.

as: (1) common—for all students; (2) alternative—for identifiable groups of students; and (3) individualized curricular elements.

Having identified three discrete curricular elements for each subject area, it is then possible to talk about individualizing the curriculum in a more explicit manner. Individualizing the *common curricular elements* is a matter of pacing, intensity, and repetition; the structuring of the original presentation; and the structuring of subsequent practice. There is, however, a definable standard of achievement which all students are expected to master, although the rate and timing of such mastery will vary from student to student. In the case of the *alternative curricular elements,* the decision will be made on the basis of student interest and ability as to which of several curricular alternatives is appropriate for any one student. The process of individualization in this case revolves around two dimensions: the selection of the alternative pattern for an individual and then, beyond that, the same considerations of intensity, pacing, and repetition that are found in the common curricular elements. With the *individualized curricular elements* the selection of material is left up to each student, and the process of individualization will here revolve around joint decision of the teacher and student as to the means of attack, the depth of the investigation, the appropriate extent of study, the elements contributing a reasonable expectation for competence in the subject, and finally a specific program designed to cover the agreed-upon material. All students will be expected to have a part of their study in each subject area devoted to an individualized curriculum. The nature of the topics investigated and the depth of study would of course vary depending on the ability and interest level of the student involved. That is, each student should be encouraged to use the skills he has developed in an area of his interest and concern. The statement "individualizing the curriculum" in this context takes on a wide meaning and at the same time provides a specific policy framework for curriculum decisions.

> 3. *In each subject area several groups of students whose
> needs are sufficiently distinct to require a discrete
> program of studies can be identified.*

It must be quickly added, following assumption 2 above, that
while all pupils should study continuously in all the above subjects,
the proportion of time devoted to a particular subject, the distribution of that time, and the nature of the content selected from that
field ought to vary according to the needs of each individual and to
the social demands that his goals, aspirations, abilities, and circumstances require. Thus while there should be a set of common
requirements, defined in terms of levels of growth,[1] each pupil's
program should be planned for him and be uniquely his own. Each
subject-matter field would provide for several different groups of
pupils. Grade-level distinctions may well disappear.[2] Groups of
students may be identified in such a way as to suggest continuous
progress, defined subject by subject and student by student.[3] One
recommended set of categories for grouping pupils is[4]:

> Limited
> Comprehensive—low interest
> Comprehensive—high interest
> Subject-talented—low interest
> Subject-talented—high interest
> Gifted
> Remedial

Variations more appropriate to specific subject-matter areas can
be developed.

A student is expected to be placed in different groups for different subjects. Furthermore, additional allowance for meeting indi-

---

[1] Levels of growth refer to extent of mastery of common curricular elements defined
for each subject area. For a more complete discussion see assumption 4 in this chapter.
[2] The Melbourne High School, Melbourne, Florida, under the creative leadership
of B. Frank Brown, is an example of such a school at present.
[3] Such a proposal has been developed by Edwin A. Read of Brigham Young University.
[4] See Chap. 6.

vidual needs would be provided within each group. In addition to presentations common to all students in a group, or to students of more than one group, and discussion opportunities with students of like interests and abilities, the individual study program would require the identification of unique interests and abilities and programs of study developed by and for each student as a part of his systematic course work. The proportion of students in each group will vary from school to school.

Grouping of pupils increases the possibilities for individualizing both teaching and learning. When based on reliable and valid appraisals of student achievement levels, potentials, and interests related to the particular course, grouping can promote excellence and reduce failure. Policy should recognize that pupils' achievements and interests fluctuate, and that even their abilities change. Grouping practice, therefore, must permit earned transfer from one group to another as measurement of student progress justifies. Thus groups in the new design remain tentative and are reviewed and altered by the team in each subject area in the regular course of evaluation.

Teaching members of the team must be involved in grouping decisions; thus special training equipping them to adapt course structure and methods to special groups becomes important. Since some teachers are more talented as the leaders of one kind of group than others are, these variations in teachers' skills and interests become important factors contributing to the achievement of predicted values of grouping.

Before going on to assumption 4, it might be instructive to note the evolution of student grouping. The grouping of students is as old as the school itself, and certain specific grouping procedures have appeared fairly consistently throughout history. The most universal grouping phenomenon is that of selection. Selection assumes that the nature of the institution is already determined, and the students must then be "selected" on the basis of their ability to meet the criteria of the institution itself. As the growth and development of secondary education in the United States is considered, many such special-purpose institutions which have selected students on the basis of predetermined and readily determinable criteria are noted. At about the turn of the century, two things occurred to put new focus on this policy of student grouping. High school education, which has been an important public option for some fifty years in the United States, rapidly evolved into a pattern of compulsory school attendance. Also, just after World War I, educational testing gained popularity, and these tests provided schools with additional criteria for the grouping of students. The legacy of this pattern still exists in polytechnical and commercial high schools in the major cities of the country. In essence, the data from educational testing programs were used to categorize students in appropriate programs of study, and students were automatically placed in these courses of study as a result of the testing programs. Whether or not the school facility was separate, the course of study remained fairly well departmentalized for each group of students.

In the 1930s a vigorous reaction to this rigid system occurred, most significantly in the elementary school, but more visibly in the secondary school. Renewed commitment to the comprehensive high school arose. Emphasis was switched to a common program for all students, and equal educational opportunity was stressed. Grouping of students was rejected as being undemocratic. Again in the 1940s there was a reaction to the common program as teachers and the public became dissatisfied with the educational results which they attributed to the great difference of ability in any one class. Special classes for the able students and remedial classes were organized. Often administrators did so without giving official notice to the public; and, in some instances, homogeneous sections were not even noted on the official time schedule for the school in fear of public reaction to this "lack" of common educational experience.

The decade of the 1950s was marked with a rousing defense of ability groupings, but instead of ability grouping by total curricula as had been done in the 1920s, ability grouping went forth course by course. Administrators recognized that a student's ability is not necessarily equal across all courses of the curriculum.

It is the proposal of the new design that this process of the 1950s be refined even further in the 1960s. To this end, the establishment of "activity grouping" is suggested. Within any given course some activities are appropriate for a wide range of student abilities and interests, and other activities are appropriately reserved for students of more homogeneous selection. For example, a class in social studies might convene to listen to the President's inaugural address, or to witness a man in orbital flight. Both these activities would be appropriate for students in widely varied grades, and of different interests and abilities. Following this common activity presentation the students might well be divided into groups representing different kinds of ability and interests; these groups might meet for discussion, for debates, and for other kinds of educational processes associated with the basic presented material.

4. *Each subject, when properly taught, will include four basic types of instruction.*

Any subject, properly conceived and properly taught, will include four kinds of instruction: Some kinds of instruction can be carried on more effectively in large groups; other kinds of teaching require small-group instruction; certain topics and pupils will probably require a considerable amount of independent and individual instruction; and all subjects will require special laboratory instruction.

Educational engineering, guided by research in the psychology of learning, provides many useful innovations in instructional procedures, innovations which the teacher of the future will integrate into course structures. For example, various types of teaching machines are presently being used in schools throughout the country. Appropriate combinations of different types of instruction necessarily will vary according to both subject-matter areas and groupings of students. The types of instruction, including examples, purposes, and required physical facilities, are detailed in Chapter 4.

5. *Adequate instruction in each subject-matter field requires senior teachers who are both well trained in their subject-matter fields and highly skilled in teaching and who are assisted by less highly trained members of the instructional and supporting staff.*

The assumption here is that in the interest of effective education, teachers should be used in the fields where they are well prepared. This contrasts with the too frequent practice of assigning teachers to perform in fields where they are not fully competent. It is well known that within any subject-matter area, teachers vary in degree of competence to lead different phases of the learning act. For example, some excel in teaching one special area of history or literature and are less competent in other necessary parts of these subjects. Some are superior as lecturers to large groups; others do especially well as small-group leaders. Outstanding teachers of writing or grammar may be quite weak as instructors of oral or speech skills. Teachers also differ in the breadth and depth of their mastery of a particular domain of knowledge, in their degree of professional commitment and interest, and in their leadership potential, i.e., supervisory and planning abilities. Failure to identify, recognize, and utilize these staff differences in staff assignments can be wasteful of human energy—both the teachers' and the students'.

Another waste of highly trained staff occurs as teachers continue to use a percentage of their energies on necessary duties which do not require professional training. Such work can be readily identified and assigned to teaching assistants and clerical staff. As teachers are trained to supervise such supporting personnel and to delegate to them routine duties, increasing effectiveness and efficiency in expenditure of time and money can be realized.

As teachers (and others) in particular domains of knowledge develop standards and procedures for identifying and assessing levels of competence, better utilization of diverse talents will result. At least three levels of teacher status will emerge—the highly talented and experienced senior teacher, the competent staff teacher of lesser experience and training, and the intern or beginner. Teams from each department will be developed. Such teams will be led by a senior teacher and comprised of staff teachers, beginning teachers, interns, teaching assistants, and clerical help. This notion of "team" is elaborated upon in Chapter 5.

> 6. *Class size, length of class meeting, and the number and spacing of classes ought to vary according to the nature and aim of the subject, the type of instruction, the level of ability and interest of the pupils, and the aim and purpose of the teaching.*

Such flexibility can be predicted to allow both the teacher and the student more efficient use of time and talent. As high schools are now organized, however, these conditions of flexibility do not prevail. A pupil, gifted or dull, is required to take mathematics for fifty-five minutes daily in a class of thirty for three full years during the full six years of secondary education. A similar requirement, varying in the number of semesters and years, is true in English, in science, in physical education, and in other subjects of the curriculum. While convenient administratively, this lockstep procedure is educationally indefensible, for little research evidence supports it.

In scheduling classes, the nature of the subject ought to be considered. These questions might be raised: Is primary emphasis upon skill or concept development? Should emphasis be placed on short periods of practice or on longer concentrated periods of study? (For example, in science, the need is for longer periods of time for laboratory, as contrasted with vocal music training in which there is no preparation period and the maximum benefit for one session may be obtained in a half hour or less.) Should the total time required to accomplish the purpose of the course be 90 minutes or 300 minutes per week?

Furthermore, some phases of instruction—the making of assignments, the administration of certain kinds of tests, the presentation of some kinds of information—can be carried on better in larger groups. Other kinds of activities, i.e., where genuine group interaction is necessary, where testing is required to determine whether or not what has been taught has really been absorbed and understood, require a group of ten or fifteen pupils involved in a discussion if the teaching is to be effective. In still other instances the pupil does not need to be under a teacher's direction nor does he need to be taught in a group. He should be spending his time alone reading, writing, memorizing, or drilling. Occasionally he might meet team members for individual conferences. It would seem that group work may not be as necessary for as much of the time as the schedule currently demands.

In time, each subject-matter field ought to have a flexible structure for its teaching, one that is appropriate for the subject, for the teachers, and for the learners. This structural variation recognizes the fact that pupils differ widely in their abilities, in their capacities, and in the pace at which they learn. Some can profitably use large blocks of time working relatively independently; others need to be directed more closely. Certain students may even need constant supervision and, in terms of their attention span and interest, require rather short periods of study with more frequent class meetings. Senior professional teachers, guided by an up-to-date body of learning theory, responsible for carrying out decisions of length, size, and spacing of their classes, should be central in making such decisions.

> 7. *It is possible to obtain scheduling assistance through the use of data-processing equipment in order to implement a large degree of schedule flexibility.*

Experience to date indicates that the use of data-processing equipment makes possible a great deal of flexibility in scheduling classes. The time is here when basic scheduling information can be listed on cards, and processed by high-speed computers. Relevant data include: the program of studies that each pupil selects, in consultation with professional staff; teachers and their appropriate assignment; rooms, their use and capacity; and other special data. Class lists, teacher assignments, pupil and room schedules, as well as the master schedule can be generated by machine implementing carefully prescribed educational policies. Research in progress at Stanford University involving both educators and industrial engineers and research at other institutions clearly demonstrate the value of data-processing equipment in a wide variety of applications beyond scheduling. In any event, practical assistance in master schedule construction for cooperating schools *is* available now,[1] and pupil assignment by machine to predetermined schedules has been possible for some time.

[1] The master schedules for several pioneer schools have been constructed by the Stanford High School Flexible Scheduling and Curriculum Study. They are all operating on a modular schedule involving up to 105 period modules per week. Cooperating schools are Homestead High School, Fremont Union High School District, Sunnyvale, California; Lincoln High School, Lincoln Unified School District, Stockton, California; Marshall High School, Portland Public Schools, Portland, Oregon; and Virgin Valley High School, Clark County, Nevada.

3

A MODEL FOR
CURRICULUM PLANNING

The planning of a curriculum requires the selection of alternatives. Scarce resources—time, facilities, teachers, and students—must be allocated, and all subject offerings compete for these resources. The reasons for allocating resources are not always clear, and even when clear, limits to their rationality usually exist. As for the physical facilities, ideally form should follow function. Practically, the wisdom of elders and sometimes ancients, frozen in masonry and brick, to a large degree controls functional possibilities. There are also logistical considerations of schedule construction. The important dimension may be either the ease of casting a program into last year's mold or the necessity of accommodating a bus schedule, and legal requirements must always be honored.

Perhaps the most powerful limiting forces controlling the quest for more effective educational programs derive from traditions, traditions which define a series of interlocking expectations: expectations of parents, of students, of teachers, of school board members, and of the community as a whole. Tradition decrees, for example, the source of financial support and often the amount; the length of the school day and school year; the number and organization of classes; standard teaching load, class size, and teacher-pupil ratio; the use of auxiliary staff; subjects to be included in the required and the elective parts of the curriculum; and requirements for employment, for admission to schools of higher education, for credits, and for Carnegie units.

It is important to distinguish between those limitations about which nothing can be done and those which may be overcome. A model for curriculum planning encourages the consideration of alternatives to traditional course structures, class sizes, use of staff, number and spacing of classes, total time which should be allocated to any one class, or even alternatives to the necessity of a daily schedule.

The Concept of the Curriculum as a Function of Area

The entire curriculum can be thought of as an *area* to be scheduled. The horizontal dimension represents the number of students, the vertical dimension represents the length of time in the schedule module.[1] If the school has 1,800 students and the school day lasts from 8 A.M. to 4 P.M., the curriculum area could be shown as below:

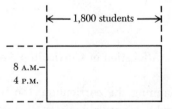

The area of the curriculum when a daily schedule module is used.

8 A.M.–
4 P.M.

←— 1,800 students —→

---

[1] A *schedule module* is that period of time during which the master schedule does not repeat itself. For example, in conventional schedules the schedule module is one day; in the example described the schedule module is one week.

If a weekly schedule is used, the curriculum area becomes that area shown as follows:

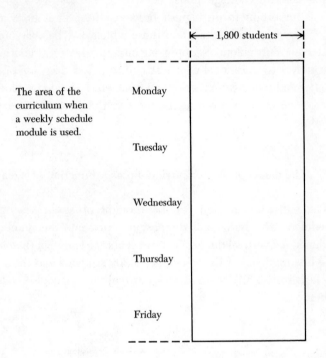

The area of the curriculum when a weekly schedule module is used.

1,800 students

Monday

Tuesday

Wednesday

Thursday

Friday

Allocation of Curriculum Area to Subject Fields

In planning the curriculum, the total curricular area (derived from total time available times the total enrollment) is available for scheduling for whatever purposes may be desired. Allocation of this time to specific purposes is illustrated graphically as follows:

Number of students

	Lunch
	Faculty meetings
Time	Individual study
	Available for direct instruction

The allocation of the total modules available for each subject-matter field will result from extended planning. It will be based upon requirements imposed upon the department, consideration of the ability of the student population, customs, and the desires of the department itself as to what it wishes to offer.

Number of students

	Lunch
	Faculty meetings
Time	Individual study
	The arts · *English* · *For. lang.* · *Math.* · *Nat. sci.* · *Phys. educ.* · *Soc. sci.* · *Guidance*

After each subject of the curriculum has been allocated an area, the design of each course (called the course structure) may then be formulated. Factors similar to those used in allocating time and students to the curricular area will be taken into consideration in the formulation of an appropriate structure for each course in the subject field.

The Concept of Modular Units in Curriculum Planning

The curriculum, conceived as an area to be scheduled, is made up of subparts called modular units which are derived from units of time, units of class size, and units of course structure. The modular unit of *time* chosen should be the largest amount of time, multiples of which will give period lengths desired for any instructional purpose. If 40-minute, 60-minute, or 120-minute classes are desired, a 20-minute module would be appropriate. The modular unit of *class size* selected should also be the minimum size desired for any instructional purpose. Class size need only be estimated by modules, whereas period length is precisely determined by the time module selected. A 10-student module would accommodate classes of approximately 10, 20, 30, 40, etc. Though any modular unit can be selected for either period length or class size, it is desirable to select as large a modular unit appropriate to reduce the complexity of scheduling, yet small enough to achieve desired flexibility. If we select a module of 15 students meeting for ½ hour, our basic module can be represented as an area.

15 students

½ hour   ▯   Scale: 15 students = ⅛ in. width
                      ½ hour = ¼ in. length

Thus a "class"[1] of 30 students meeting for an hour (a conventional class unit) would appear as a multiple of the modular unit:

[1] A *class* is a scheduled meeting of a section of specific students and instructional staff meeting at a specific time and place.

30 students (2 modules)

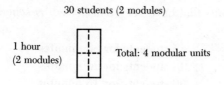

1 hour
(2 modules)   Total: 4 modular units

A wide variety of structures is possible, all multiples of the basic modular unit:

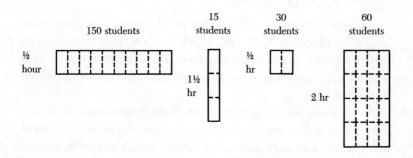

150 students

15 students

30 students

60 students

½ hour

1½ hr

½ hr

2 hr

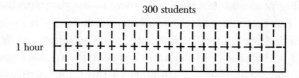

300 students

1 hour

Note that many other basic modular units are possible:

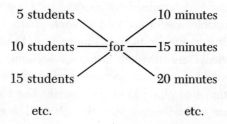

5 students   10 minutes

10 students ——— for ——— 15 minutes

15 students   20 minutes

etc.   etc.

Modular units that have been considered by school districts for planning are:

15 students for 30 minutes
15 students for 20 minutes
30 students for 15 minutes
15 students for 25 minutes
10 students for 10 minutes

The smaller the modular units, the greater the flexibility—but also the greater the complexity.

Course Structure   The concept of course structure is depicted in diagrams 1, 2, and 3, which show how students and instructors in a given course may meet during a time cycle (such as a week). A structure consists of phases and sections, defined as follows:

Phase: Each phase is a subdivision of the structure for which students, instructors, and period length remain constant. We have adopted the convention of using capital letters to denote phases. Each phase, in alphabetical order, is equal to or smaller than the preceding phase in class size. The rows of the diagrams illustrate phases. For example, phase A in diagram 1 involves all students in one meeting for a specific time interval. The difference between phase B and phase C in diagram 1 is that the sections need not involve the same group of students or the same instructor. The vertical scale of diagram 1 indicates length of the class meeting.

Section: Each section is a subdivision of a phase. Numerically subscripted lowercase letters denote sections. The number of sections in a phase is determined by dividing total course enrollment by the permissible size of sections in each phase. In phase A in diagram 1, all students are in the same section. In phase B in diagram 1, students are divided into two sections; in phase D, students are divided into four sections, and so on. Hence one may speak of section 1 of phase D of this course. The horizontal scale in this diagram indicates class size, though each section may have some permissible variation in size.

Modular Course Structures

The module used for these examples is 15 students meeting for ½ hour. All section sizes and lengths are given in multiples of this module.

Diagram 1: The course structure for 240 students in English consists of five hours of instruction each week in phases A through E. Phases A through D meet once a week, phase E meets twice weekly. Phase A has one section of 240 students meeting for ½ hour (time module). Phases B and C each have two sections meeting for ½ hour with 120 students (8 student modules) each. Though phases B and C have identical structures, they are designated as separate phases because student and teacher combinations are not the same. Phase D has four 60-student sections meeting for 1½ hours. Section E has sixteen 15-student sections meeting twice weekly for 1 hour. Phases A, B, and C are used for large-group instruction, phase D for laboratory and writing activities, and phase E for small-group instruction.

DIAGRAM 1. SUGGESTED STRUCTURE
FOR AN ENGLISH COURSE

A	a															
B	b_1								b_1							
C	c_1								c_1							
D	d_1				d_2				d_3				d_4			
E	e_1	e_2	e_3	e_4	e_5	e_6	e_7	e_8	e_9	e_{10}	e_{11}	e_{12}	e_{13}	e_{14}	e_{15}	e_{16}
	e_1	e_2	e_3	e_4	e_5	e_6	e_7	e_8	e_9	e_{10}	e_{11}	e_{12}	e_{13}	e_{14}	e_{15}	e_{16}

Diagram 2: This modern language course for 120 students with 5 hours instruction a week has three phases. Phase A consists of two sections of 60 students meeting for ½ hour five times per week. Phase B has four sections of 30 students meeting twice weekly for 1 hour. Phase C is unscheduled; i.e., students are allowed ½ hour a week for individual and independent study.

Diagram 3: Shorthand for 120 students is taught in two phases for 5 hours of instruction, nine meetings a week. In phase A all 120 students meet together for 1 hour once a week. Phase B, ½-hour practice sessions, may be scheduled morning and afternoon on the remaining four days of the week for a total of 8 meetings.

DIAGRAM 2. SUGGESTED STRUCTURE   DIAGRAM 3. SUGGESTED STRUCTURE FOR
FOR A MODERN LANGUAGE COURSE   A SHORTHAND COURSE

a_1	a_2	

(Diagram 2, Phase A: five rows of a_1 | a_2; Phase B: two rows of b_1 | b_2 | b_3 | b_4; Phase C: unscheduled)

(Diagram 3, Phase a: one cell a; Phase b: eight rows of b_1 | b_2 | b_3 | b_4)

Planning Course Structure

Given a specific number of students to be scheduled for a certain period of time, a wide variety of course structures is possible. There may be limits, upward and downward, to class size. Staff limitations, in terms of both time available and competence, figure prominently. Scheduling limitations also present an important source of constricture (e.g., the time available for any one course may be limited by a number of factors).

In this first example, 300 students are scheduled into a course for five hours per week:

EXAMPLE 1

ELEVENTH-GRADE U.S. HISTORY

300 students (20 modules)

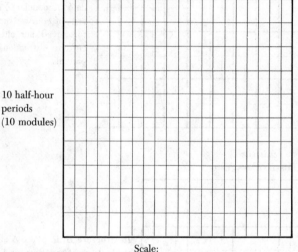

10 half-hour
periods
(10 modules)

This is the total
modular area
allocated for this
course (which
might be in any
teaching field).

Scale:
⅛ in. = 15 students
¼ in. = 1 period

Within the same scheduling area, several different structures could be planned in a flexible schedule, without encroaching on the scheduled time for any other subject.

To provide for different interest and ability groups of students and to allow for greater flexibility in the total curriculum offered, it is possible and educationally desirable to schedule courses with different total time allocation. These arrangements are shown in Examples 2 and 3.

EXAMPLE 1

COURSE STRUCTURE I

CONVENTIONAL STRUCTURE

300 students

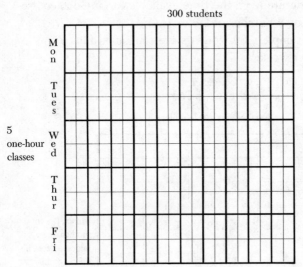

5
one-hour
classes

This class of 300 is divided into ten classes of 30 students meeting one hour daily. A modular concept of course structure need not alter current instructional patterns.

EXAMPLE 1

COURSE STRUCTURE II

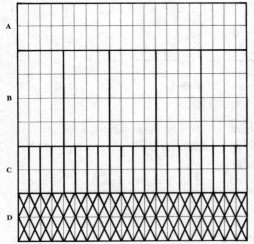

In structure II, in phase A all 300 students meet together for 1 hour for large-group instruction.

In B the group is broken into 5 sections of 60 students each, to meet for 2 hours for a research laboratory period.

There are, in C, 20 classes of 15 students per class, meeting for 1 hour of small-group instruction.

Finally, in D, 1 hour of individual study is provided.

EXAMPLE 1
COURSE STRUCTURE III

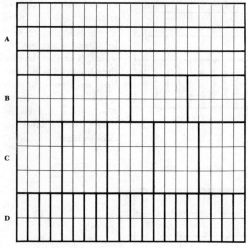

In structure III, 300 students meet together for 3 half-hour periods of large-group instruction (phase A).

In B, four classes of 75 students per class meet for 1 hour of large-group instruction grouped by ability and interest level.

In C, 5 classes of 60 students each meet in laboratory sessions for 1½ hours.

Phase D shows 20 classes of 15 students each, meeting for 1 hour of small-group instruction.

EXAMPLE 1
COURSE STRUCTURE IV

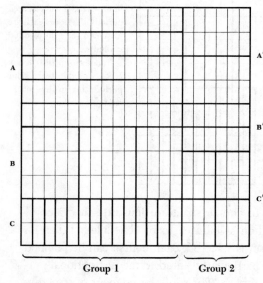

In structure IV, the class of 300 is divided into two groups by ability level or other criteria:

Group 1 consists of 210 students. In Phase A these 210 students meet for one period. In phase B group 1 is divided into three groups of 75, 75, and 60 students meeting for three periods of lab instruction. In phase C there are 14 classes of 15 students each meeting for two periods of small-group instruction.

Group 2 consists of 90 students, meeting for two large-group sessions of two periods each (phase A′). Phase B′ shows two large-group sessions of one period each. Phase C′ shows a set of two classes of 45 students each for two lab sessions of two periods each.

EXAMPLE 2

5
half-hour
modules
(total
time
2½
hours)

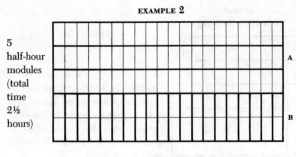

In example 2, a class of 300 students meets as a group for three half-hour lectures, and in small groups of 15 students each for classes of one-hour duration. Note that the total time involved is substantially less than is currently typical. It is not known how much such a time reduction would affect student learning.

EXAMPLE 3

14
half-hour
modules
(total
time
7 hours)

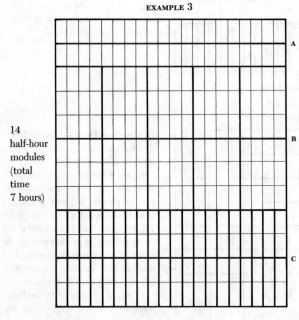

In example 3, a class of 300 students meets in two large groups for one-half hour each. Two research periods of 2 hours each are provided for groups of 60 students.

Small-group instruction is scheduled in two 1-hour periods for groups of 15 students each.

The wide variations in course structure illustrate the value of thinking of the curriculum as an area to be scheduled. When an appropriate modular unit is selected, each course can be planned with a structure that is particularly suited to the instructional purpose it is trying to accomplish. The modular concept of structure does not necessarily require any structural change from the conventional practice as is indicated by structure 1, where the five hours of class meetings during the week for 300 students can still be scheduled as 5 one-hour meetings, each meeting at the same time on subsequent days. It does permit, as structures 2, 3, and 4 illustrate, a break from current practice without changing the total time allocated. Examples 2 and 3 suggest that as we examine our instructional purposes, variations in total time allocations as well as variations in structure may well be productive. In one sense, schools have always had a modular system of scheduling. However, with a more appropriate size of module and by considering the curriculum as an *area* to be scheduled, many variations in structure are possible.

In the models described here, two distinct kinds of problems require resolution: those of scheduling and those of curricular requirements. The curricular decision is one of concluding just what courses will be taken by which students, how much time will be allocated to each, and the appropriate structure of each course. The problem of scheduling must be solved by the fitting together of the pieces that result when a variety of course structures is adopted. When the curriculum is considered as a function of area made up of small modular units, it becomes easier to consider the possibility of altering the total amount of time to be allocated to any one course. Some courses may meet for ten periods a week, some for fifteen periods, and some for as few as three periods a week. While it may be difficult to fit together a wide variety of structural patterns into a single master schedule by hand, electronic computers are available to assist with schedule construction.

It is useful—and interesting—to identify some of the curricular assumptions which are made to accommodate current schedule rigidity. When one group of curriculum experts was consulted and asked the question, "How would you schedule your subject, or courses in your subject, if you had complete freedom to schedule them in any way you wish?" over 80 per cent of the answers mentioned some variation of thirty students meeting for a class hour. In some instances, double periods were suggested; it was also suggested that two or more classes be combined for certain purposes. It was certainly quite clear, however, that the traditional base of thirty students meeting for one hour was accepted with little question. Later, after a curriculum module of fifteen students meeting for one-half hour had been suggested, and after several of the structures indicated above were discussed with this same group, the experts were again asked to develop ideal instructional patterns for each of their subjects. This time less than 5 per cent of the suggested classes called for thirty students meeting for one hour, or variations of this standard pattern. Experts, answering in this fashion, suggest that we may unwittingly limit the number of alternatives from which we select the course structures which will be implemented in school curriculums. Viewing the curriculum as an area consisting of modular units offers a means of overcoming limitations of many curricular "givens" which are imposed by the sheer force of tradition.

At this time it is impossible to state how learning would be affected if the instructional time in any one subject were increased or decreased. Limited evidence exists to suggest that the number of class hours a subject is scheduled may not be nearly as critical as often supposed. Evidence exists to suggest also that different uses of instructional time should be considered and that there should be systematic experimentation with course structure. Thinking of the curriculum as a function of area—as an *area* to be scheduled—is one means of systematically considering a wider range of alternatives.

Since the evidence is meager as to efficiency of learning as a function of the amount of time a course meets and as a function of the way in which meetings are scheduled, experimentation with different patterns is desirable in order to obtain such evidence. The models here presented make it easier to provide variations within a given time allocation.

4

TYPES AND PURPOSES
OF INSTRUCTION

Types of Instruction

Instruction in each subject-matter field consists of four basic types which are defined as follows:

Independent and Individual Study (IS)[1]   Instruction in which the student engages in activities independent of other students and in large part independent of immediate teacher direction is independent study. Examples are reading, writing, drill, research, conferences, memorization, working with teaching-machine programs or other automatic instructional devices. Note that IS may well take place as one phase of laboratory instruction. The purposes of this type of instruction are to promote independence, to provide opportunity for study under optimum conditions, to provide opportunity for study of topics beyond the regular curriculum, and to permit maximum use of instructional resources.

This notion of independent study is not new. The school has not been the customary setting of such study, however, for most secondary school policies are based on the assumption that students will loaf or indulge in malpractice or skulduggery if not continually supervised. Administrative decrees, made necessary by fears of legal

---

[1] For each type of instruction abbreviations have been indicated which will be used subsequently to refer to each type of instruction.

liability, support the supposition that in-school learning which is not supervised by a licensed teacher is almost certain to be either ineffective, or if effective, bad or unsafe for tender adolescents. Although teachers and administrators value and admire responsible self-direction in students, they rarely encourage the expression of this trait in a school setting. Yet teaching students to study individually and without close supervision will pay permanent dividends without jeopardizing the school's responsibilities *in loco parentis.*

Independent study requires a library, a laboratory, a study room, or an individual study alcove. Special self-study equipment includes records, tapes, tape recorders, teaching machines, microfilms and projectors, a variety of reading-improvement devices, and library-reference resources. Effective use of many of these learning tools requires time for individual study, careful planning by the teacher, and constant reappraisal by the staff.

Small Group (SG)   In small-group instruction the primary emphasis is on face-to-face contact and group interaction. Analytical or exploratory discussions and group critiques demand limited numbers. Small-group interaction provides opportunity for individual participation, for discussing ideas raised in large-group or laboratory discussion, for establishing close teacher-pupil relationships, and for testing effectiveness of large-group and laboratory instruction. Thus to be defined as "small-group instruction," the group must be small enough for all members to interact (i.e., a group composed of from five to fifteen members).

Leadership of small groups often requires teachers highly trained in this special kind of instruction. Yet some small groups can function well and achieve much when led by students. The opportunity for developing student leadership in the small group is great, especially when grouping reveals different kinds of leadership talent among the students.

The only required physical facilities for small-group instruction are small rooms with flexible tables and movable chairs.

Laboratory (LAB)[1]   Laboratory as here defined includes those physical facilities for which special equipment and tools are needed to enable students to work independently and in small groups and to practice skills, to experiment, and to apply ideas suggested in large-group instruction. Examples of such laboratories are libraries, playing fields and gymnasiums, office-machine centers, music practice rooms, instructional materials production centers, audio-lingual language rooms, science-research laboratories, reading-skills laboratories, study centers, machine shops, etc.

Large Group (LG)   Large-group instruction in the new design is that which, because it involves a large number of students, places primary emphasis on presenting materials with a minimum of interaction. Illustrated lectures by the teacher or a guest speaker, the making of assignments, testing, televised lessons, and motion pictures are a few of its uses. The purposes of having large-group instruction are these: to conserve teaching time; to improve the quality of the presentation; to make effective use of resource persons; to capitalize on special talents of staff; to make efficient use of motion picture, television, and other audio-visual aids; and to use equipment and facilities efficiently.

A most important aspect of large-group instruction is the "mass media" nature of its communication patterns. The techniques and variety of effects are powerful, and the results can be both good and bad. This imposes tremendous responsibilities on the teacher who conducts the large-group sessions. Included in his highly specialized skills must be the ability to teach his audience to examine critically as well as to appreciate the advantages and the limitations of mass media communication. He must especially help his audience to understand the complementary relationships and

---

[1] Although the laboratory is not a "basic type of instruction" in the same sense that SG, LG, IS are (viz., the lab as defined here is not units of people), it was felt that the inclusion of laboratory as a "type of instruction" is justified on the grounds that it includes each and all three of the other "types of instruction" but from a different structural base.

differences between large-group and small-group communication patterns. It is unwarranted, however, to conclude that students cannot be "involved" individually in large-group presentations. Such involvement is usually "mental" or passive, but may be as vigorous as overt participation in small groups or individual conference situations.

Required physical facilities for large-group instruction are comfortable fixed chairs with tablet arms, moderate elevation, permanently installed instructional aids, and provision for light control.

Purpose of Instruction

The type of instruction that is selected will depend upon the educational purpose. The proposed instructional pattern differs from the conventional pattern mainly in its emphasis on independent study and laboratory work, and assumes facilities not now commonly provided. These facilities include study alcoves as well as laboratories or resource centers for mathematics, social sciences, and other studies including the humanities. Most secondary schools now have libraries and laboratories for science, and many have laboratories for language and reading.

Under the proposed arrangements, a student would spend part of his school life in large groups in which material would be presented by a teacher who had been given substantial time to prepare his presentation, and who would be especially qualified for making that presentation. Some testing and routine administrational duties would go forth in the large group. Although the effectiveness of large-group instruction has been demonstrated, further evaluations are needed by teachers and administrators using this approach.

Effective small-group instruction is particularly difficult to achieve. Too often small groups are achieved at great effort and large expenditure of staff, time, and room resources only to be conducted by the teacher in such a way as to make the number of students present an irrelevant factor. It must be stressed that small-group instruction and large-group instruction refer to a *type of instructional pattern* not merely to the number of students.

Students would learn some skills in laboratory situations and other skills by practice on tapes and autoinstructional devices. Students would have greater responsibility for their own learning, becoming more competent in self-directed study. Individual study would not need to be completely academic. A boy or girl might attend school in the morning and work on community projects or in a paid position in the afternoon. Not all students can profit from a full day of instruction; some may need outside work or other outlets for their energies and talents. The differentiation of pupil groupings and types of instruction needed for effective teaching will require an extended program of guidance. Such a program is discussed in Chapter 7.

In any domain of subject matter, effective integration of the four types of instruction requires team teaching guided by staff planning. Imposition of any pattern of large-group, small-group, and individual study assignments without staff planning can be disappointing in its consequences. Particularly important is the fact that not all teachers, even though very competent in traditional classes of thirty pupils, can quickly adjust to large-group responsibilities. Another important matter, one requiring faculty planning before inauguration of new course structure, relates to necessary changes in staff-load standards. It is most important that participating teachers understand and accept these changes. These problems will be further examined in Chapter 5.

5

STAFF UTILIZATION

The implementation of the new design for high school education requires changes in the present concept of high school staff. Three principal categories of staff are needed: professional, supporting, and resource personnel.

The professional staff in any one subject-matter area includes senior teachers responsible for curriculum design, for major instructional duties, and for staff assignment and other administrational tasks. These senior teachers will be assisted by staff teachers who will take limited responsibility for the conceptual outline of courses, will assist with curriculum development, and will take substantial instructional responsibility. The professional staff also includes "intern" teachers and beginning teachers. These neophytes assume responsibilities for curriculum assistance, for instruction, and for administrative details. Other staff having professional status in the school-personnel structure are the specialists who serve all departmental areas—librarians, psychometrists, psychologists, counselors, deans, and medical personnel, for example. Changes in the structure of the teaching staff also require new concepts and adjustments in the roles of these specialists.

The professional staff should be supplemented by less highly trained personnel, such as teaching assistants, clerks, technical assistants, and proctors. Each member of this supporting staff would be trained in a specific area of competence. For example, teaching assistants, although they may have no professional training in teaching, might well have college degrees in the subjects in which they are assisting. The advantage of this concept of supporting staff is that it identifies personnel functions in the school which do not require the breadth of training necessary for a fully qualified teacher.

Resource personnel from other professions and special fields will also be brought into the school to assist with certain special functions.

Professional Staff

The Senior Teacher   The senior teacher is the heart of the school. He (or she) is an experienced and mature person who has had substantial graduate work both in the academic area he is teaching and in professional education. He holds an M.A. degree, perhaps the doctorate. He is a highly paid professional, employed on a twelve-month contract. Senior teachers take major responsibility for leadership in curriculum design in their specialized field, assign staff, assume major instructional responsibility themselves, and participate in appropriate local, state, and national organizations. They are responsible for any or all of the four types of instruction (see Chapter 4) and may spend substantial portions of time in large-group, small-group, and laboratory instruction as well as in directing individual work. Senior teachers also must work with the other teachers and interns to assist them with their professional growth. Teacher education institutions may well use senior teachers as "clinical professors," or in a similar consultant capacity.

Senior teachers must define specific standards in their various fields which ultimately will make possible licensing of those qualified to carry out the general responsibilities listed above. As a starting point, dimensions of these standards might include: (1) evidence of successful experience in handling the full range of instruction unique to the field; (2) evidence of consistent professional growth, growth measured by utilization of and contribution to relevant research and innovation; (3) evidence of effective staff leadership; (4) evidence of familiarity with a body of theory which integrates content and method; and finally (5) evidence of a desire and the energy to accept the professional commitment of senior-teacher responsibilities.

Each department in the school may have as few as one or as many as three or four of these senior teachers.

Staff Teachers   The largest proportion of the professional staff is made up of regular teachers (staff teachers). Such teachers hold M.A. degrees in education or in the subject field in which they are teaching and have some training beyond the bachelor's level in their subject field. In a school of 1,800 pupils, each subject area will have from four to nine regular teachers each of whom will have one or more areas of specialization within the general subject field. These teachers work with the senior teachers to design the courses, have some responsibility to assist with curriculum development, and take substantial instructional responsibility. Staff teachers may appropriately be responsible for any of the four major types of instruction. They may work either full or part time and serve on twelve, nine, or fewer months' contracts.

The majority of the professional staff will be licensed as competent practitioners by their own boards in each field. Standards will recognize and encourage high levels of specialization in specific areas of subject matter as well as in different types of instruction. Levels of achievement of these standards will guide departments in planning team assignments in which teachers may achieve optimal satisfaction and reward in work which best utilizes their unique talents and demonstrated experience.

Many staff teachers will excel senior teachers in specific types of instruction and will prefer concentration in these specialties rather than acceptance of broader responsibilities demanded of the senior teacher. In accepting concentration, staff teachers become more free to focus their energies on teaching strengths which promise greatest service to students; and they leave areas in which they are weak to fellow specialists.

First-year Teachers   First-year teachers are considered to be roughly equivalent to intern teachers in terms of the types of responsibility they would be given, though they might carry a heavier individual load than would interns.

The need to achieve more intelligent induction of beginning teachers has long been recognized. Traditionally staff-utilization practices tend to limit the possibilities for appropriate initial experience for the new teacher. Very frequently the beginner faces a load assignment matching that of experienced teachers, a load often aggravated by some of the more difficult and shunned assignments which experienced personnel have finally escaped. The beginner sinks or swims doing, as best he can, nearly everything that experienced teachers do. The beginner has been often isolated from opportunities to communicate with experienced staff who could help him in many ways.

The staff structure of the new design solves some of these problems of staff induction. The important beginning years will thus be predictably more productive of professional growth and of better service to students. Fewer promising young teachers will leave the profession disillusioned and disappointed by their induction experiences. Experienced teachers will find more useful ways to accept their proper responsibilities and opportunities to train beginners.

Intern Teachers   Interns are teachers engaged in a fifth year of college or university preparation who are required to teach in the schools in conjunction with their program of formal training. They have responsibility for some curriculum assistance and are expected to perform major instructional duties in any of the four types of instruction. They may be responsible for certain administrative details of classes, for keeping records, and for other tasks requiring some professional competence. Perhaps interns should be used most cautiously for small-group instruction since this less-structured situation is one for which preparation is most difficult.

Supporting Staff

Teaching Assistants   Teaching assistants are persons who have a sufficient degree of expertise in the subject matter to be of substantial assistance to the professional staff but who are not fully prepared as teachers. They are usually employed as part-time staff members. Under the direction of the professional staff they assume instructional responsibility in laboratory and research assignments, correct papers, and work with individual students and with small groups. They are especially helpful in compiling that research which serves as the basis of large-group lectures. Similarly, teachers may ask teaching assistants to compile lists of proposed projects or proposed topics of investigation for able or slow students. The effective use of the teaching assistant will depend, of course, on the imagination of the teacher using his services.

Teaching assistants typically will have a bachelor's degree in the subject in which they assist. It is important to note that they are *not* clerical assistants. They should properly be used to perform tasks related to their academic preparation. Often they are persons who have other responsibilities and are interested in only part-time employment. Housewives with older children are perhaps the most effective general source of teaching-assistant personnel when the position is defined on a part-time basis. They enjoy the creative challenge which is free from the many responsibilities of full-time employment which takes them away from home too extensively. School districts which have had experience with teaching assistants report that they obtain a better caliber of person when they employ them on a part-time rather than on a full-time basis, thus using persons who do not have to rely solely on the teaching-assistant income for a livelihood.

Technical Assistants   Technical assistants have specific, nonprofessional skills important to the school program. Graphic arts skills are perhaps the most frequently needed. Where television or other mechanical equipment is used in the program, technical assistants may be employed to operate or maintain such equipment. Their employment becomes increasingly necessary as the sophistication and complexity of school equipment becomes greater; no longer can the school afford to rely on a general three-unit course in audio-visual aids to turn the teacher into a general-purpose operating and maintenance technician. Technical assistants will often be college-trained in their specialties, though the level of competence will vary widely with the specific assignment. In some instances, custodial personnel have been trained as technical assistants quite successfully.

Clerical Assistants   Clerical assistants are persons skilled in typewriting, clerical, and stenographic duties. They may work with teaching machines, materials and programs, proctor students in situations requiring monitoring rather than teaching, and perform other routine nonprofessional chores in the classroom, such as taking attendance. Such personnel may or may not have had college training, although increasingly it becomes desirable for them to complete at least two years of community college as a requisite for employment as clerical assistants.

Prior to employment of teaching assistants and clerical and technical assistants, certain decisions involving professional staff must be made. The role expected of the assistant in a specific context must be clearly defined. To that end, these questions might be asked: What is the assistant expected to do, and to whom is he responsible? How does his work relate to the teacher's work? What changes in the teacher's role are necessary? How do teachers perceive these changes and react to them? Once these and other questions are answered it becomes important to define standards for selection of competent assistants, including the role of the teacher in the selection of supporting staff, and to develop careful coordination of their activities. In addition, procedures for evaluation of the assistant's performance should be anticipated. And perhaps teachers will need training in how to supervise and use constructively the assistants assigned to help them. Finally, space and tools necessary to the performance of assistants' duties must not be overlooked.

Resource Personnel

Resource personnel are specialists from the professions and specialized fields who may be working either in the school system or, more typically, in the community. They are drawn upon to help with a particular course or to assist in other ways with the school program. Resource personnel have full-time staff assignment in the school, a part-time responsibility, or make only an occasional visit on an informal basis. Examples of such personnel are psychometrists, librarians, psychologists, physicians, lawyers, newspaper editors, and engineers.

Staff Classification Problems

Effective teaching is facilitated through the use of a differentiated staff which works as a team. Certain problems, however, exist concomitantly. For example, although the distinction between intern teacher, teaching assistant, and clerical assistant is fairly easy to make, the distinction between senior teacher and staff teacher may at times be extremely difficult to make. It may be necessary to give the title of senior teacher, for reasons of longevity, to persons who would never reach such positions on the basis of their training and performance, under present systems. Despite such difficulties predicted for staff classification in the new design, it is to be noted that under prevailing conditions injustices are now perpetuated in assuming that all teachers are equal except for differences in years of service and of formal scholastic preparation.

One possible way to deal with the problem of achieving professional acceptance of senior teacher, staff teacher, and beginner or intern classifications is suggested by the "grandfather clause" approach. By assigning senior-teacher status to all currently tenured staff and requiring that new teachers earn this status, much personal anxiety and staff opposition can be relieved. Retirement will gradually solve many problems, too. This approach has disadvantages, but they, however, would not exceed the disadvantages of perpetuating present practices and injustices. An alternative approach would be to provide obvious differentiations in responsibilities or terms of service as justification for salary recognition. This approach would encourage all professional staff to serve for eleven months— an encouragement which would lead to increased professional effectiveness because teachers would have additional time for preparation and study.

In implementing a new design for high school education, some school districts may wish to make finer distinctions in staff responsibilities in these proposed categories whereas other districts may prefer to make fewer distinctions. The new design does not require any set staff hierarchy but rather advocates that it is necessary to make better use of the most effective and highly trained members of school staffs if programs are to be improved to a significant degree.

Team Teaching

The integration of professional staff, support staff, and resource personnel into a productive unit to carry out a particular course cycle *creates* a teaching team. Such functional groups, organized for an educational purpose, are not new: The new design simply requires different kinds of teams—teams which will better utilize human and material resources at less cost per unit of productivity.

When developed by effective planning related to specific operational and personnel situations, teaching teams can achieve these advantages:

1. Optimal use of strength and maximum support of weakness of available professional staff.

2. More equitable access to teaching specialists by all students in a particular course or area of instruction.

3. Encouragement of *activity grouping*, rather than course or curriculum grouping, by providing an integrated personnel structure for a given course.

4. Better adaptation of teaching resources to groupings of students, thereby facilitating improved services for all ability levels.

5. Improved communication and cooperation among teachers of a particular department, fostering departmental cohesiveness, morale, and professional growth.

6. Improved interdepartmental communication and cooperation, especially where cross-subject-matter teams come into being.

7. Better utilization of those powerful student resources which contribute to the learning and teaching experience. Student teams, modeled after able teacher teams, can be encouraged. Thus students realize more clearly their own responsibilities and opportunities to contribute.

8. For students, practical examples of methods by which diverse talents, skills, and beliefs can contribute to organized group efforts. The common problems of all areas of industrial, political, and social life can be dealt with more intelligently if students are familiar

with team-teaching and team-learning structures and processes.

9. Reduced use of professional staff to perform routine duties.

10. Better utilization and adaptation of material resources, buildings, equipment, mechanical aids, and electronic services.

The processes by which teams are organized will determine to a large degree whether predicted values are achieved. Teams should be organized in specific contexts for unique purposes, purposes not always transferrable as exact patterns from department to department, or from school to school. Variables which limit and define team-teaching opportunities include all the familiar personnel, curriculum design, school facilities, and finance variables, none of which can be ignored, in a particular school program.

These guidelines will be helpful to administrators and others seeking to improve staff utilization by team-teaching innovations:

1. Team teaching is not necessarily the best approach for all purposes and in all situations.

2. Professional staff responsible for action as team members must be involved in these sequential stages of action:

   a. Decisions as to specific purposes of the team.

   b. Planning, which involves appraisal of all available human and material resources relevant to purposes, as well as an opportunity to participate in their selection; assessment of various alternatives for structure and organization including predicted consequences related to purposes and costs; and clear understanding of the plan adopted.

  c. Carrying out the plan.

  d. Evaluating the results.

3. Adequate planning and evaluation takes time and energy. This time must be made available to teachers as part of their regular load—not in addition to it. Failure of administrators to recognize this can jeopardize the whole operation. In addition to time, suitable places to plan and evaluate must be provided.

4. All roles defined for both professional and nonprofessional staff must be clearly understood. Communication must assure that individual role expectations match these definitions, and that defined roles do not require competencies not possessed by, or trainable in, participating staff. Training, when necessary, should occur in advance of practice.

5. New team organizations commonly clash with deeply ingrained concepts of staff load. New guidelines, different for various departments and types of instruction, must evolve from experience and replace traditional load standards. Clerical and teacher-assistant loads also require careful appraisal, but are more difficult to estimate because of lack of precedent. All loads may be expected to vary in different subject-matter and course phases. Also, they change along with the variance of the schools' educational engineering, those technical services provided to relieve staff of former duties. Failure to attend to new load definitions, or to permit flexibility according to different types of instruction, can seriously impair realization of team-teaching values.

6. Team members' daily or weekly schedules must per-

mit strategically placed evaluation meetings. In some situations these meetings should occur daily, in others semiweekly or once a week. Research services, to assist practicing staff in accurately assessing both gains and costs[1] related to established purposes, are very important in the achievement of responsible professional growth in team-teaching skills.

7. Leadership in the development of teaching teams has the responsibility to deal with personal needs and anxieties of the school staff affected. Changes in well-established roles of older teachers commonly involve personal costs. Efforts to reduce these costs contribute to success potential. Certain informal factors affect costs, too, and should be assessed in team assignment decisions. For example, some teachers work better together than others for reasons not always associated with formal role competence. To the extent teachers perceive team innovations as threatening or overly costly, leadership will find willing, intelligent participation difficult to achieve. Professional unity in public interpretations of the innovation will also be lacking, as well.

8. All school innovations, including team teaching, are subject to public scrutiny. Leadership must recognize the necessity for public understanding and yet resist inexpert public interference with professional decisions. Information made available to the public must stress the advantages related to better education and efficiency. Here research and evaluation become a valuable necessity; here also the students themselves can play a very important role.

[1] Costs here refer to the psychological factors which must be assessed.

9. It must be recognized that there is no such thing as team teaching per se. Team teaching is an approach to instruction. Its success or failure may hinge on a number of factors—personnel, facilities, organization of course material, course structure, schedule demands, load factors, grouping of students, and many others. Success and failure must be determined in terms of individual combinations of such factors. Global judgments about the success or failure of "team teaching" as such are never justified.

Determining Staff Requirements

Staff requirements will be developed through an arbitration of ideal staff as determined by curriculum design and practical limitations of facilities and finance. Figure 5.1 indicates the guidelines used in computing staff requirements for the present model. The definition of staff load is in the same half-hour periods used throughout this example and is estimated for all staff members at 80 half-hour periods. These guidelines are for the purpose of estimating staff needs only, and actual individual staff assignments will differ considerably from these guidelines.

Eight categories of staff responsibility have been defined in Figure 5.1. For the teacher, all these are oriented to classroom responsibility. The allocation of all but classroom time is purely arbitrary, though a rationale exists for the proposed division. The increased emphasis on staff meetings is necessary because of the different types of staff involved, as well as the greater emphasis on staff coordination. The minimal emphasis on the correction of student materials reflects the availability of teaching assistants to carry the major share of this responsibility. Specific time has been allocated for evaluation and for parent and student conferences. Note

FIGURE 5.1. COMPUTATION OF WEEKLY STAFF LOAD

**An illustrative guideline to be worked out in detail
by each school and by each department**

	Teacher	Intern	Teach. asst.	Clerical assts. and tech. assts.
1. Classroom presentation, preparation, and evaluation	50°	54	60	
2. Guidance instruction	5	5	0	
3. Staff meetings— faculty and departmental meetings, staff coordination, and curriculum development	8	8	8	Allocated as desired
4. Correction of student material	3	3		
5. Evaluation—instruction, course content, and staff utilization	6	2	2	
6. Conference—student and parent	6	4	2	
7. Supervision of students— out of class	2	2	4	
8. Clerical	0	2	4	
Total load	80	80	80	80

Load factor assignment for different types of instruction:

Large-group instruction 2 to 1   Laboratory 1 to 1
Small-group instruction 1.5 to 1   Individual study 1 to 1

Teacher equivalents:

Teacher equals 1 teacher   Teaching assistant equals ½ teacher
Intern equals ⅔ teacher   Clerk equals ⅗ teacher

° All figures shown are in half-hour periods.

the very small amount of time allocated for the out-of-class supervision of students, and note also the expectation that teachers will not perform any purely clerical duties. As for the interns, their duties parallel those of the teacher with some greater emphasis on classroom presentation and preparation and less time spent in evaluation and conference. The load of the teaching assistant is defined in Figure 5.1 for those teaching assistants who have *instructional* loads. Teaching assistants who are used to conduct research for teacher presentations and to correct materials would have an individually defined load as do the clerks, although it is expected that there would be a substantial differentiation in teaching-assistant and clerical responsibilities.

In this illustration (Figure 5.1), staff load has been kept constant for all subject areas. This need not be the case. It may well be that for each subject area a different general staff-load index will be appropriately developed. However, for a theoretical example, it was felt that a general staff-load index for all subjects would suffice as a point of departure.

At the bottom of Figure 5.1 appears a load-time allocation for different types of instruction, showing that for large-group instruction a ratio of 2 to 1 is suggested. In other words, for each one period assigned for large-group instruction, two periods should be allocated for load purposes. For small-group instruction a ratio of 1.5 to 1 is necessary, and for laboratory and individual work a ratio of 1 to 1. This ratio assumes that preparation for laboratory instruction is minimal outside the laboratory session itself. It should be noted that this is an instructional load ratio, that support staff can be assigned in addition. For example, if a teacher were assigned to a laboratory class, with a 1 to 1 ratio for his load, it would mean that he could be assigned to a total of fifty periods, or twenty-five hours of laboratory instruction during the week. If this actually were his load, it would be a very difficult type of load to maintain without support staff. Sufficient teaching assistants, however, would be available so that the teacher would have time for preparation and other aspects of his duty *within* the assigned class time. But it is not anticipated that any one teacher would be assigned such an extreme load; actual staff assignments would usually involve varied types of instruction. Finally, as mentioned before, the use of teaching assistants in noninstructional assignments would radically alter the apportionment of their (teaching-assistant) time. The assumption here is that a sixty-period instructional assignment would be for those teaching assistants who were used primarily in laboratory groups and as support personnel in instruction positions.

At the bottom of Figure 5.1 is an entry called teacher equivalents, where, for the computation of budget and financial obligation, it is estimated that an intern could be hired for approximately two-thirds of the salary of the teacher; a teaching assistant for about one-half the salary of a teacher; and a clerk for about two-fifths the salary of a teacher. Hence, to determine the available staff in terms of teacher equivalents is to enable a department to determine what proportions of staff it wishes to employ, given a specified level of financial support.

Figure 5.2 shows how the computation of staff load is translated into specific staff needs for mathematics. The number of classroom periods assigned to each type of personnel and the teacher-equivalents factor assignment shown in Figure 5.1 make possible the computation of the staff factor ratio in Figure 5.2. Figure 5.2 is a summary table which can be constructed only after course structures have been determined and staffing patterns decided. All staff requests are categorized by instructional type and by staff classification. The heading "Total staff modules" refers to the number of period modules of time required in each category. Total staff factors result from the multiplication of total staff modules by the instruction weight ratio, explained above. Staff factor ratio is a constant multiplier which helps in computing teacher equivalents. It is composed of two parts: the proportion of a full-time assignment for the category of staff member that is represented by *one* period, multiplied by the proportion of a teacher's salary a full-time

FIGURE 5.2

SUBJECT AREA: MATHEMATICS

		Category of staff*	Total staff modules	Instruction weight ratio	Total staff factors	Staff factor ratio	Teacher equivalents Instruction	Teacher equivalents Support
LARGE GROUP	Instruction	T	120	2	240	0.020	4.80	XX
		I		2		0.012		XX
		TA	40	2	80	0.008	0.64	XX
	Support	TA	20	XX	20	0.008	XX	0.16
		T-C	50	XX	50	0.005	XX	0.25
		TOTALS			390		5.44	0.41
LABORATORY	Instruction	T	56	1	56	0.020	1.10	XX
		I	150	1	150	0.012	1.80	XX
		TA	221	1	221	0.008	1.77	XX
	Support	TA	20	XX	20	0.008	XX	0.16
		T-C	100	XX	100	0.005	XX	0.50
		TOTALS			547		4.67	0.66

SMALL GROUP	Instruction	T	35	1.5	52.5	0.020	1.05	XX
		I		1.5		0.012		XX
		TA		1.5		0.008		XX
	Support	TA		XX		0.008	XX	
		T-C		XX		0.005	XX	
		TOTALS			52.5		1.05	
INDIVIDUAL† WORK	Instruction	T	8	1	8	0.020	0.16	XX
		I				0.012		XX
		TA				0.008		XX
	Support	TA		XX		0.008	XX	
		T-C		XX		0.005	XX	
		TOTALS			8		0.16	
		GRAND TOTALS			997.5		11.32	1.07

°T: Teacher
I: Intern
TA: Teaching assistant
T-C: Clerk or technical assistant
† In addition to formally assigned individual study, each staff member has provision in his total load for unassigned individual study responsibilities.

person in the given staff classification would normally receive.[1] Teacher equivalents (staff factors × staff factor ratio) are divided into two categories: instruction and support. Total teacher equivalents reflect a number of administrative decisions which have been taken into consideration in developing the staff factor ratio (see Figure 5.1). Data are tabulated in two ways: teacher equivalents, the financial obligation for the instructional program, and total staff factors, the actual total work load.

The instruction weight ratio is obtained from Figure 5.2. For large groups this ratio is 2 to 1; for small groups, 1.5 to 1; and laboratory and individual work is entered at 1 to 1. A multiplication of the total staff modules by the instruction weight ratio gives the total staff factors. For support staff there is no weight ratio. If a teacher is responsible for 50 instructional periods, each period would constitute 1/50 or 0.020 of a full load for that teacher. This proportion, 0.020, is multiplied by the teacher-equivalent factor. For a teacher this would be 1, which would give a staff factor ratio of 0.020. For an intern the staff factor ratio would be computed on the basis of each instructional period's being 1/54 of the total load, and this resultant would be multiplied by 2/3 to give the ratio 0.012. The teaching assistant's ratio would be computed on the basis of each period's being 1/60 of a total load, which would be multiplied by 1/2 (the proportion of teaching equivalents for the teaching assistant), which gives the staff factor ratio 0.008. The multiplication of the total staff factors by the staff factor ratio gives the teacher equivalent for instruction and/or support, depending on the line. The addition of the large-group, small-group, laboratory, and individual work gives a grand total which indicates the total number of teacher

---

[1] If 54 factors are considered a full-time instructional load for one intern, then one factor would represent 1/54 or 0.0185 of a full-time load. If an intern is considered two-thirds of a teacher equivalent, then to change intern instructional responsibility to teacher equivalents, it must be multiplied by 0.6667. Both reciprocals can be combined in advance so that a single multiplication is possible (0.0185 × 0.6667 = 0.0123). 0.012 becomes the intern staff factor ratio.

equivalents needed. In mathematics, for example (Figure 5.2), this total is equal to twelve teachers.

The actual staff would consist of seven teachers and the equivalent of three full-time interns, six full-time teaching assistants, and two full-time clerks. More persons would be involved as interns, teaching assistants, and clerks because these staff members would not typically be responsible for full-time loads. Some staff teachers could also be hired on a part-time basis, depending on personnel available.

This table facilitates the assignment of additional staff members and indicates, in a gross way, just where curtailment of staff might be possible. The table is not intended as a rigorous formula and must be interpreted in individual situations and with professional judgment. Each school must ultimately determine its own staffing formula, adding, perhaps, distinctions between senior teachers and staff teachers or between technical assistants and clerks. Also obvious is the fact that staffing formulas represent averages from which there are bound to be wide variations.

6

COURSE REQUIREMENTS
AND GROUPING OF STUDENTS

The purpose of establishing course requirements is to provide students and teachers with an educational program which is as effective and efficient as possible. The same is true for building course structures and functions and for formulating grouping criteria.

How much time should a student spend in class? How much of this time should be consumed by formal instruction and how much by seminar-type discussion and individual laboratory work? How much time should be devoted to individual study? The answers to these questions are difficult indeed; moreover, educators have long doubted that the answers should be the same for all pupils.

We assume that students can learn more and learn more rapidly if given proper instruction and opportunity. Too many students, because of their overloaded schedules, have gaps in their education, especially in art, music, and practical skills. Some students currently take very little or no mathematics or science because they cannot compete with college-bound students in courses as "elementary" as introductory algebra and chemistry I. For others, creative gifts in the applied arts and crafts of our culture lie dormant because no regular instruction is given in these areas. Students might well be able to fill in these gaps if courses were added to the schedule and scheduled on other than a daily basis.

Assuming a flexible schedule, several possible approaches may be taken to a new design for high school education. The one on which this particular proposal for curriculum change is based specifies that all students take courses in each curriculum field but with individualized programs of study in each subject. To implement this new design, groups of pupils with differing personal needs and potentials must be identified in each subject area. With such grouping, acceleration, remediation, enrichment, and drill all would be possible, leading, predictably, to more efficient learning than that in traditional programs.

It is proposed that groups be formed on the basis of two primary variables: first, *ability* and level of growth in the particular subject area; and secondly, developable *interest* in its study. This concept of groups leads to the establishment of four basic groups *in each subject area:* a *comprehensive low-interest group* (a group with satisfactory though not outstanding ability, and with low interest); a second *comprehensive* group, with *high interest* in the subject; a third group of *subject-talented* students with *little interest;* and a fourth group of *subject-talented* students with *high interest.* In addition, in some subject areas provision should be made (and would be made) for handling groups of gifted students and groups of remedial students or students of limited ability. These additional groups would vary from subject to subject.

The assumption is made that in any given academic subject area, valid and reliable procedures for determining each student's present level of achievement, abilities, and interests exist. Among the more useful indicators of these traits are:

1. Intelligence tests and aptitude test batteries
2. Achievement tests
3. Observations made by previous teachers
4. Interest inventories
5. Expressed desires of students and parents related to the above

Professional teachers in each subject-matter area should participate in decisions about how best to identify student groupings according to aptitudes, abilities, and interests as they are related to their own specialties. The recommendations of professionals may not always be compatible with similar classifications made by parents and students. Bases for decision must be supportable by expert experience, a body of theory, and must be clearly interpreted to all those affected.

Procedures also must recognize that achievement, measured ability, and interest traits are variables responding to teaching and learning. Transfer from one grouping classification to another, therefore, should be readily possible as new levels of ability and interests blossom or old patterns fade, as they will. Further, groupings appropriate to foster excellent teaching and learning in one subject-matter area are not necessarily equally appropriate in another department. Even within one course, groupings useful in one phase of the total-course cycle may be inappropriate in the next phase. For some specific activities no grouping at all may be the best decision.

The new design stresses the importance of that flexibility which recognizes the uniqueness of each subject area in serving individuality in students. Therefore, it would be unwise to impose on all subjects—irrespective of special purposes, requirements, and functions—the same grouping patterns. Before grouping decisions are made in any school, the precise purposes and aims of each subject and of the total school should be defined, and the ability and interest levels describing its student body evaluated. The next step requires departmental leadership to establish the minimum course objectives. These become the common objectives of all students, and, once established, departmental leadership involves the staff of specialists in deciding what groupings of students, if any, will best facilitate the achievement of these objectives and what variations in course structure and phases in course cycles will best serve each grouping.

Building on this basic common structure for all, departments next plan additional courses and suitable variations which will give maximal service to those unique differences in student talents and interests. Such courses define the varied educational diet by which each department builds diverse student talents.

Basic groupings, offered as guidelines for such departmental study, are given below. They reflect gross distinctions of alternative curriculum elements. The groups may well be combined for certain activities which reflect common curriculum elements, and provide only the structure and not the substance for individualized aspects of the curriculum, as was discussed in assumption 4, in Chapter 2.

Basic Groupings for Each Subject[1]

Arts—visual, performing, and practical

Comprehensive
   a. Low interest
   b. High interest
Subject-talented and interested
Gifted

Language—English

English remedial
   a. Writing
   b. Reading
   c. Speaking
   d. Non-English-speaking
Comprehensive
   a. Low interest
   b. High interest
Subject-talented
   a. Low interest
   b. High interest
Limited ability

Language—foreign

Comprehensive
   a. Low interest
   b. High interest
Subject-talented
   a. Low interest
   b. High interest
Limited ability

Mathematics

Remedial
Comprehensive
   a. Low interest
   b. High interest
Subject-talented
   a. Low interest
   b. High interest
Mathematics-gifted
Limited ability

---

[1] These groupings reflect the recommendations of curriculum study groups. The differences between area groupings ("language—foreign" has no remedial or subject-talented category, whereas "mathematics" does) reflect the opinions of each curriculum study group.

Natural science

Comprehensive
  a. Low interest
  b. High interest

Subject-talented
  a. Low interest
  b. High interest

Science-gifted

Limited ability

Physical education

Physically handicapped and inept

Comprehensive
  a. Low interest
  b. High interest

Subject-talented
  a. Low interest
  b. High interest

Gifted

Social science

Comprehensive
  a. Low interest
  b. High interest

Subject-talented
  a. Low interest
  b. High interest

Social-science-gifted

Limited ability

These classifications should be defined and described in greater detail for a particular school program. Departments may find the following guidelines helpful in doing this:

Remedial   The remedial student is one for whom there is the specific expectation of a higher level of performance. He is so far below the normal range in the subject that it is impossible for him to cope with the materials that are a regular part of the curriculum, despite his measured ability to do so.

Comprehensive   Students with ability and achievement levels to handle adequately the required sequence in a given subject. Those with high interest, capable of minimally acceptable work in the subject, can be divided from those who are neutral or uninterested when such subgrouping can contribute to better teaching and learning.

Subject-talented   A grouping for those students with substantial ability in that subject. This group might include from 15 to

50 per cent of the students and would not be the same for each subject or school. As in the case of comprehensive classifications, subgroups based on interest variations are possible and may well be useful.

Gifted   Students endowed with some unusual talent or potential in an area. This group might range from 1 to about 10 per cent of the students; it would include only those students with a real, absorbing interest in a particular subject.

Limited talent   Students with below average potential but who, nevertheless, can develop through the use of specially planned instruction in this subject-matter area. The number of students in this category may vary from 1 to 25 per cent in a particular school or subject.

Plans as to time required to achieve course goals in each department and at each grade level must be integrated for the whole school. This integration inevitably places limits on departmental planning, yet even by accepting these limits, departments achieve freedom for creative flexibility not possible in today's traditional curriculum patterns. It is important that curriculum minimums in each subject be defined at a low enough level to allow for a substantial amount of individualization of the curriculum (to be defined subject by subject for each individual student). This means that in order to require each student to take each subject each year, the time allocated must depart substantially from the present daily one-hour pattern of instruction.

Figure 6.1 illustrates one such integration of time requirements by departments and grade levels. Once these time allocations are made, departments may develop course structures as each sees most appropriate for groups and purposes as long as such structures are kept within the time allocated. Each department may use less time; none may use more. Each has time for basic requirements for the total six-year span, and each has time for individual study and additional concentration in the departments. Departments may

FIGURE 6.1. MINIMUM REQUIREMENTS IN EACH SUBJECT—SIX-YEAR HIGH SCHOOL

Grade level	Basic time requirements for subjects:						Requirements at each grade level	Reserved for individual study	Available for concentration	Total available°
	Mathematics	Science	Social studies	English and foreign language	Practical, visual, & performance arts	Physical education				
7	7	5	5	12	8	7	44	8	8	60
8	7	5	5	12	6	6	41	10	9	60
9	5	7	5	10	5	6	38	12	10	60
10	5	5	5	10	5	4	34	12	14	60
11	3	5	5	8	3	4	28	14	18	60
12	3	3	5	8	3	3	25	16	19	60
Total minimum requirements	30	30	30	60	30	30	210	72	78	360
Typical total minimums now	30	20	45	50	20	60	225	0	135	360

° Equivalent to a 6-period instructional day (12 half-hour periods times 5 days of instruction equals 60 periods available weekly for the year).

Notes:
1. All times shown are number of ½-hour periods per week required.
2. In addition to required minimums, a total of 12 periods (over the 6 years) equals a single concentration; 24 periods equal a double concentration; and 38 periods are added for a gifted program. Normally, college preparatory students will be subject-talented and will take additional concentrations in mathematics, science, social science, and language. Subject-talented and interested students will usually take a double concentration in the subject. Students gifted in a particular subject will usually take the gifted program, but not usually in more than one subject.

reduce the minimum requirements, shifting time saved to periods for elective concentration, as long as they (the departments) do not exceed the total time both reserved for them and available to the individual student each year. The curriculum-planning model developed in Chapter 3 is a useful framework for this modification.

Every student would study in all subjects every year, but the basic time requirement for such study would be low. For example, it is recommended that as few as ninety minutes per week be spent on some subjects by some students during some years. The aims and purposes for each group in each subject must be defined; equally important is the decision as to how much total time each subject should have. This means deciding how long students should spend in instruction in fields where both their talent and morale were low. While most subjects would probably require at least three half-hour periods a week, the distribution of the ninety minutes will grow out of the "what" to be taught. Even this ninety minutes may prove to be an excessive requirement for those limited students for whom we seek only to maintain minimal skills.

The basic requirements apply, in general, to students who are included in the comprehensive, low-interest group for that particular subject—students capable of a basic satisfactory performance in a given subject. Since these requirements are low, time is left for specialization and concentration according to individual needs. In this way all students would study in each of the subject fields in the curriculum but not for an equal amount of time.

In addition to required minimums, students in a number of groups will experience substantially larger amounts of instruction and intelligently planned variations in individual study during the school day, week, and year. Figure 6.1 well illustrates this. Note how the time available for individual study and for concentrating in specialized fields increases as the students progress toward the senior year. Notice how certain subjects show little change in time allocation over the six years, while others are concentrated at the beginning or in the middle of the six-year sequence.

Departments may vary concentrations from one extra period per week beyond basic requirements to the maximum periods reserved for student concentration and/or individual study, depending upon the individual student's needs, abilities, interests, and aims. Here guidance services seek to help each student understand the various departmental concentrations offered, to relate them to his own situation, and to answer the question, "At this stage of my educational program, what is the best decision as to use of available time for concentration and individual study?"

To assist departments in planning, three additional concentrations of study are arbitrarily suggested:

1. A single concentration. This consists of an additional *twelve* periods of instruction spread (not necessarily evenly) over the six-year period of high school. This might be appropriate

   a. For comprehensive students with high interest in the subject matter, or

   b. For subject-talented students who are not particularly interested in the subject matter.

2. A double concentration. This consists of *twenty-four periods* of instruction in addition to the recommended minimum spead over the six-year period, and may be appropriate for subject-talented students who have high interest in the subject matter.

3. A gifted concentration. This consists of *forty-eight periods* of instruction beyond the required minimum, and may be taken by students of outstanding subject ability and intense interest in the subject.

Figure 6.2 illustrates how one mathematics department might plan concentrations for different groups at different grade levels over the six-year span for a school of 1,800 with 300 at each grade level. Note that a gifted student in mathematics may commit his total available concentration time to mathematics alone. He thereby must give up possible concentrations in other subjects, unless he is counseled to devote some of the 72 periods of individual study during his six-year program to this purpose.

Additional Notes on Basic Subject Requirements It may appear upon a first examination of Figure 6.1 that the total amount of time available for any given subject has been reduced below that now provided in schools. But bear in mind that this is the *minimum* requirement and that concentrations are built on this foundation so that a substantial number of students may take *more* than this. Figure 6.1 represents the common basic program for students with minimum ability and interest, not the total opportunity offered for each subject. All pupils would seek more than this in some subject areas. In addition, the new design assumes a different structure of course time with the assumption that when time is more nearly tailored to individual course requirements, relatively less time will be necessary to attain the same level of student performance.

The assumption in this illustration is that the total minimum requirements over the six-year periods will be thirty periods in each subject except language. This means 210 out of a possible 360 periods are required. One-third of the curricular instructional time is not yet accounted for in the minimum requirements and remains for allocation on the basis of a student's interests and abilities.[1]

English and foreign language have a fairly heavy concentration of requirements: in grades 7 and 8, twelve periods each; down to ten in grades 9 and 10; and reduced further to eight periods in grades 11 and 12. Forty-four out of the sixty periods available

[1] Some problems need to be considered in terms of college-admission credits. These 360 half-hour periods equal 180 one-hour periods. Dividing by 5, the result is 36, or 6 units a year, which is typical of present patterns. For purposes of Carnegie unit equivalents, 7 to 8 periods a week would yield 1 unit of credit per year, 4 periods a week would be equivalent to ½ unit per year. It is anticipated that college credit requirements would be changed if evidence is gathered supporting alternative college-admission patterns.

FIGURE 6.2. WORK SHEET—PERIOD REQUIREMENTS FOR DIFFERENT SUBJECT GROUPS AT EACH GRADE LEVEL

Subject: <u>Mathematics</u>

GROUPS TO BE PROVIDED FOR

	I Base group comprehensive low interest		II Comprehensive high interest		III Subject-talented low interest		IV Subject-talented high interest		V Gifted		VI Limited ability		VII Remedial*	
	No. of periods	No. of students	No. of periods	No. of students	No. of periods	No. of students	No. of periods	No. of students	No. of periods	No. of students	No. of periods	No. of students	No. of periods	No. of students
Total periods base required	30	xx	30	xx	30	xx	30	xx	30	xx	18	xx	15	xx
Additional concentration	0	xx	12	xx	12	xx	24	xx	48	xx	0	xx	0	xx
Total periods to be scheduled	30	xx	42	xx	42	xx	54	xx	78	xx	18	xx	15	xx

Grades:														
7	7	90	7	30	8	105	8	15	10	15	3	15	12	30
8	7	105	7	30	8	105	8	15	10	15	3	15	12	15
9	5	105	8	30	7	90	10	30	10	15	3	15	10	15
10	5	105	8	30	7	105	10	'30	10	15	3	15		
11	3	105	6	30	6	105	10	30	18	15	3	15		
12	3	105	6	30	6	105	8	30	20	15	3	15		
Total periods	30	xx	42	xx	42	xx	54	xx	78	xx	18	xx		xx
Average number of students	xx	103	xx	30	xx	102	xx	25	xx	15	xx	15	xx	10

° Usually, the 15-period concentration for students needing remedial instruction will be concentrated in grades 7 to 9 and *is added* to group I requirements.

71

would be prescribed at the seventh grade. This is reduced to twenty-five periods prescribed out of the sixty available at the twelfth-grade level. The balance would be planned according to the need of the student. Single concentrations of twelve additional periods, the additional possibility of a double concentration of twenty-four periods, and forty-eight periods for gifted students could be given to an individual student as desired.

The 72-unit provision for individual or independent study is spread out (rather arbitrarily, for the illustrative purpose here) over six years. But it *is* included in a six-hour instructional school day. It may well be desirable to spread this over a longer school day and to incorporate "homework" time into the instructional framework. Greater availability of material as well as staff resources to provide assistance to students would be requisite for such lengthening incorporation. The amount of independent study arranged for a particular pupil and the years when it would occur would be highly individualized.

Two kinds of independent and individual study are envisioned: (1) that which is planned for inclusion within a particular subject field (e.g., as a pupil takes foreign language or English, a part of the work that he plans should be independent study related to that subject); (2) that which is used by a student for various subjects according to his developing interests. In each of these kinds of independent study further distinctions of scheduled and unscheduled individual study exist. An individual might, for example, be left relatively free to go wherever he wished—to the library, to the language laboratory, to the mathematics laboratory, or to the science laboratory. At other times he and other students might be scheduled in an assigned study laboratory where groups of sixty, seventy, or eighty students would work under supervision. Both types of study are appropriate inasmuch as some students need to be supervised much of the time, others not at all. The amount of supervision needed will also vary with grade level. The time is overdue to recognize that twelfth-grade students may appropriately be treated differently from, say, seventh-grade students insofar as need for supervision is concerned. The emphasis should be on developing students' responsibility systematically rather than demanding a metamorphosis at the time of college entrance or vocational employment.

Currently many activities which are really independent-study activities, because of the demands of equipment, have to be planned only within the context of the classroom. The 20 per cent allowance for individual study within the framework of the day in the new design makes it possible for the student to have facilities available beyond a formal class context. Study-skill sessions beyond scheduled class time may be scheduled weekly in the laboratory. This independent-study idea introduces a flexibility within the school day which gives the student easy access to equipment. This also makes possible different kinds of demands in what is now referred to as "homework" as well as a redefinition of what subjects are "academic," a distinction which is now based almost solely on the assignment of "homework."[1]

The flexibility of courses and groupings as described adds new dimensions and responsibilities to guidance services of the school. The new design considerably expands the range of alternatives available to students and teachers at each grade level. But alternatives mean nothing if freedom to choose leads to decisions based on whims instead of on reliable information. Chapter 7 develops the guidance implications of the new design.

[1] Perhaps the best example of this arbitrary custom is the field of music, an academic subject long before the social studies were incorporated into the curriculum.

7

GUIDANCE

A successful secondary school program that seeks to group and regroup pupils according to their developing abilities and interests, that capitalizes upon and grows out of the work the pupil has done in the elementary school, and that hopes to join forces with the family in projecting appropriate vocational and academic goals will require a strong guidance program. In the new design for high school education presented here, note that guidance is one of the seven basic fields proposed for continuous attention in *instruction* (see Chapter 2, page 7). This means that guidance would be one of the instructional departments in the school, with suitable staff and curriculum. While this guidance curriculum would probably consist of more individual work than the curriculum in other subjects would, it would also include large- and small-group instruction where appropriate.

As in all basic subject-matter areas, definition of purposes must precede and continually guide new designs of structure and function. Guidance purposes, perhaps more than those of any other area of the curriculum, tend to be misunderstood or are at least seen as widely different by teachers, students, guidance specialists, parents, and others. Therefore, each school should carefully define the purpose of guidance in the context of the entire school operation. In the new design the basic purpose of guidance is seen to be this: *to ensure the individualization of high school education to all students with all kinds of abilities and from all backgrounds.* The new design prescribes discrete dual responsibilities for the guidance staff: to provide individual student services to support the instructional staff by diagnosing academic and vocational alternatives and developing therapeutic programs consistent with guidance staff competence; and to provide a systematic instructional program in guidance areas such as school orientation, academic program alternatives, vocational descriptions, available pupil personnel services, test interpretation, and criteria for college and university selection. This instructional responsibility has traditionally not been effective in guidance programs in secondary schools, partially because of scheduling difficulties.

The Guidance Staff

Basically, the new design for guidance involves a differentiation of guidance roles parallel to the differentiation of general staff roles outlined in Chapter 6. The guidance staff will be composed of psychologists, psychiatrists, psychometrists, counselors, specialists such as speech pathologists and audiologists, clerical assistants, technical assistants, and teacher-composed advisement teams. Each of these staff functions is clearly different. But all can be grouped under three major categories: counseling and therapy, advisement, and instruction. Counseling and therapy are so well differentiated that an elaborate discussion in this context is unnecessary. It is important to note, however, that the counseling and therapy aspects of counseling require personnel with highly specialized training. It is quite inappropriate for these duties to be performed by teacher-counselors who have minimal guidance training beyond standard teacher preparation. Even within the general area of counseling and therapy, there are requisite specializations, as for example in speech pathology and psychometry.

Advisement is a very different consideration. Teachers—instructional specialists—can and should perform this function for a majority of students. The only students who should be academically advised by the professional counseling staff are those with complex individual problems. Therefore, the new design calls for teacher-advisors whose guidance functions are narrowly defined and limited to the selection of academic programs of study and to the knowledge of the advisee as a person. The concern is to build a personal rapport between student and advisor which is only possible if relatively few advisees are assigned to any one advisor. To ensure the desired continuity, an association of advisors into advisement teams is recommended.

The heart of the advisement function is carried by the *advisement team*. Each advisement team is composed of two members of the instructional staff, teachers who share responsibility for sixty students throughout these students' years in the secondary school. Each member of the team will thus have continuous responsibility for about thirty students. The distribution of responsibility between the two teachers will vary according to their own resources, the nature of the groups assigned to them, and the planning of the grade-level group to which they belong. The student-advisor assignments and reassignments are the responsibility of a *guidance coordinator* and his staff. The guidance coordinator has the additional responsibility for selecting and developing the advisement team itself. Stability and compatibility are the twin hallmarks of the advisement team. Insofar as possible, these teams should be comprised of teachers who are unlikely to leave the school at the same time, for many guidance programs founder when staff turnover belies the theoretical assumption of advisement continuity. The compatibility of interests, the complement of competencies of the advisement team members and their mutual rapport are also important considerations. And although each member of the advisement team will have a substantial individual responsibility for a group of thirty students, there will be opportunity for combining the advisement groups of both members so that students will have, in essence, an auxiliary advisor who will provide advisement if the primary advisor leaves the staff.

Again it must be stressed that students retain the same advisement team for their total secondary school experience. Each team member is responsible for a group of students and will have continued personal contact with a second group assigned primarily to his advisement team colleague. Each team member provides a home base in the school for a particular group of students. He is their friend in court in dealing with school problems and decisions which affect them. He becomes the professional member of the school staff best informed about their personal and social characteristics, their values and aspiration levels, and their overall school achievement and growth. Because of this, the advisor has the responsibility to interpret for the school possible consequences to the members of his group of any school program, plan, or decision. The advisor does *not,* however, assume a therapeutic counseling responsibility with the student. He *knows* the student well enough to know when additional staff resources should be involved. He should alert the counseling staff to problems needing their attention. He should, likewise, alert his instructional colleagues to any special circumstances which might affect their instructional expectations of the student. He may help the student to change his program or to plan his individual course of study. He talks to each of his advisees as a friend, doing his best to gain their confidence and to get to know them well. He encourages each student and reacts to suggestions that he may make. He also takes calls from parents who are concerned about their children's program and various instructional problems.

Time will be scheduled for the team to provide for individual conferences and independent study of guidance subjects when group presence is not desired or planned by the advisement team or guidance staff. Group activities relating to advisement procedures may be developed by the advisement team itself but will usually be provided for the team by the guidance staff.

The guidance staff thus provides special services both for individual students and for the school staff. It handles specific personal problems of students upon referral by advisors, teachers, or the student himself. It provides individual and group counseling, either scheduled or unscheduled, for physical, emotional, social, and specialized academic difficulties. It administers individual and group testing programs. And it offers extensive instruction and counseling for vocational and scholastic aspirations. Furthermore, the guidance staff serves the general school staff by assisting with the definition of the total school program (including student load, setting of standards, staffing formulas, and cocurricular activities), by cooperating in curriculum development, by maintaining a referral service for students and advisees, by identifying and communicating student difficulties and special circumstances, by obtaining and furnishing normative test data, and by helping to select standard tests to be administered.

It is important to note once again that the concept of advisement is the concept of the teacher-advisor, not the teacher-counselor. The notion that a teacher with minimal training in counseling can gain the necessary competence for a major responsibility in the overall guidance program in the secondary school is firmly opposed. Conversely, it would not be unreasonable for a teacher with a depth of understanding in a specific teaching discipline and in the general academic program to offer advice and counsel to students especially interested in that discipline or who have a problem related to their academic efforts. Even when such congruity of interests of advisor and advisee cannot be identified *precisely,* assignment to advisement teams on the basis of the individual student's *general* interests is less frivolous than the completely random assignment of students to advisors, and if advisement teams are selected with complementary academic interests, a student will have systematic access to more than one point of view in the process of his program development. As is so often the case, the frustration of not being able to provide explicit distinctions has led to the abandonment of all distinctions.

Certain basic decisions must be made regarding the assignment of teachers and students to guidance groups. These important questions need answers:

1. *How shall students be assigned to guidance groups?* By sex? Grade level? At random? By interests? Abilities? What is an appropriate basis for guidance grouping? Aside from favoring coeducational groups, the new design recommends that these decisions be left to the counseling staff, which must take into consideration the interests and competencies of each advisor. In some schools, grouping according to tentative post-high school plans may be best, i.e., according to work aims, college, university, or vocational intentions. Other possibilities include grouping of some students according to areas of demonstrated special talent—science and mathematics, arts and crafts, humanities and languages, social studies, and others. Efforts should probably be made to avoid concentration of student leadership potential in any one group. The values of keeping communication open between all kinds of student talents and interests need to be kept in mind. Whatever grouping is made, labeling of students might occur, but status distinctions should be minimized. Also, provision must be made for changing advisors (see 3, below).

2. *How shall teachers be assigned to guidance groups and advisement teams?* Advisement teams should be selected to complement interests and competences of the advisors. This would provide a balance for the majority of students, who are quite undecided about their career interests and academic program. Advisement teams might often combine an experienced senior teacher with a beginning teacher or an intern. Certainly the combination of two uninterested or inexperienced teachers on one team portends unfortunate consequences. Teachers assigned to the same team should be compatible to a degree which would assure cooperative effort and mutual support. Forced team associations in advisement, as in other subject areas, generally are costly.

3. *Under what conditions should transfer of students from one guidance group to another be permitted?* Transfer will at times be desirable and may be made on the initiative of either the student or the advisement team. The welfare and effectiveness of

both the advisement team and the student are the important elements in this decision. Care must be taken to avoid using such transfers as disciplinary measures, for disciplinary problems are not usually solved in this way. No transfer should occur without the involvement and understanding of all advisement team members affected. Often parents may be consulted prior to these decisions. Students can and should learn to participate effectively and responsibly as members of many different groups of people; the advisement team's function includes modeling this kind of skill for the advisees.

The popular conception of the *counselor's* role is limited to interviewing, testing, and advising individuals. Too often the message has been conveyed that these processes require capacities, training, and understanding not possessed by classroom teachers trained only in instruction. The resulting tendency has been to confuse a proper concern for a teacher's competence in counseling with the propriety of straightforward advisement. All students are indiscriminately referred to the typically overburdened counselors. Certainly the counseling relationship does involve high levels of specialized professional training and unique competence, and, if properly handled, is important to students. However, many problems traditionally dealt with by high school counselors are not *counseling* problems at all, in the sense that special training beyond instructional competence is required. Academic advisement is the principal example.

The new design *does* require counselors for the guidance staff but limits counseling responsibilities to those students whose problems require help beyond the resources of the advisement team. Often these problems will be of such a nature that the counselor, having made a diagnosis of them, will mobilize other staff help, such as the school nurse, district psychologist, or outside professional services. But not over half of the counselor's time will be devoted to this specialty. The greater dimension of the counselor's role will be his working with teachers and student groups to achieve fuller individualization of instruction throughout the school, to define carefully the appropriate *instructional* content of the guidance program, and to prepare and present these materials as an integral part of the total instructional program.

Counselors will be responsible for the group planning of guidance services each year, for mobilizing the resources of the guidance staff to help teachers, for planning and carrying out guidance instruction for the total student body and for special groups at each grade level, and for group and individual meetings with parents and students when professional counseling services are required. The counselor will be available as a resource person to various curriculum meetings; he will supervise the maintenance of individual pupil records; he will process requests from advisement teams for data about their advisory groups; and he will evaluate the effectiveness of the use of these data. An increasing proportion of his work will be with teachers rather than with individual students.

The other members of the guidance staff are all specialists of one sort or another—psychologists, psychiatrists, psychometrists, speech pathologists and audiologists, clerical assistants, and technical assistants. These function in their conventional roles under the new design for education, and consequently their responsibilities will not be discussed here. However, it should be remarked that the professional people listed above handle the cases which are referred to them by advisors and counselors.

The Instructional Program in Guidance

Primarily because of structural limitations of class time, the instructional program in guidance has been loosely defined and largely confined either to homeroom-type situations or to time-consuming individual conferences. In the framework of the new design which allows for a wide variety of instructional modes, the instructional program in guidance can be much more fully developed. Numerous structural alternatives are possible with up to 2½ hours a week allocated to the guidance program at each grade level.

Guidance instruction might include a number of subjects which are currently incorporated in academic courses (although extraneous to the basic subject matter), which are explained upon request by teachers, or which are entirely missing from the secondary school curriculum. In these categories are such useful, and sometimes mundane, subjects as orientation in school matters, the procedures for selecting an academic program and the pupil personnel services available, and other information pertaining to the school; elementary psychology, including an introduction to the understanding of personality differences and a study of vocational alternatives, stressing the duties entailed in each occupation and the educational preparation necessary. Subjects now encountered only haphazardly by students include such vital concerns as information on colleges and universities, procedures for applying for admission, scholarship information, and facts about employment opportunities. Instruction in these areas needs to be regularized, and instruction in such things as deciding whether to attend college, choosing the right college or university, and completing applications, should be established. These topics and many others are properly taught in the guidance instruction program. In addition, formal instructional periods in guidance provide an opportunity for testing and psychometric interpretation.

One such alternative might include a half-hour daily period for guidance in which individual study could be alternated with large-group presentations by counselors, the advisement teams, and others. During the individual study periods, the advisement team could hold individual conferences with the students as needed while the remaining students, although busy studying, would be available for conferences. The large-group sessions would include presentation of systematic guidance materials in an instructional context primarily by the counselors, not the advisors—an important distinction vis-à-vis present practice.

Another structural alternative would be to schedule a 1½-hour block for the instructional program in guidance, the first hour of which would be for individual study, followed immediately by a half-hour period reserved for formal instructional presentations by the guidance staff. During the first hour the advisement team would be available for individual conferences while the remainder of the students would be free to study. A fourth and fifth half-hour period could be scheduled independently, perhaps separated by a day or two from the 1½-hour session, for the advisement team to make formal presentations or other purposes as desired. Under this arrangement the entire school might have only 1½ hours in the common guidance program; the two additional half-hour periods would be incorporated into the regular schedule. A structural advantage accrues in this arrangement in that the 1½-hour block could be used for formal testing programs or other activities for which more than a half-hour period is required. This could be scheduled as needed.

In guidance, as in all other areas, such patterns as those above are merely illustrative. Wide variation is possible within the basic framework presented. The new design adapts, for example, to those kinds of guidance problems which vary from grade to grade. Tenth-grade guidance groups may well require a distribution of the weekly hours different from that required by groups of twelfth graders. Special groups of students may be chosen for assigned additional or alternative guidance time, perhaps for group therapy or other professional services provided by the counseling staff. The instructional program and the group and individual conferences in guidance may be combined in innumerable permutations to meet the wide variety of situations which may exist in the secondary school.

Some Necessary Policy Changes in Guidance

Several basic guidance policy changes will be necessary in the secondary school.

1. The concept of "advisement team" recognizes the advisement function as being integral to the instructional responsi-

bility of the teacher specialists in each subject area. Since this is discussed in detail elsewhere in this chapter, it need not be further elaborated upon here.

2. The scope of pupil personnel services must be narrowed to those practices which are clearly relevant to the educational responsibilities of the school. The services should be limited to what can be done well, and for which staff can be provided. School publics must be informed of what school guidance *is not* as well as what it is. Professional individual therapy for students must be examined closely vis-à-vis its propriety in the general public school program.

3. Teachers must have offices suitable for interviewing parents and students and for keeping advisory group records.

4. The machine processing of pupil data is essential. Included here is the mechanization of the attendance reporting processes. The need for the vast amount of written attendance notes and cards is certainly questionable. Cumulative pupil records can be more adequately processed through data-processing techniques. Test data can be available more rapidly and with more extensive analysis. Grade reporting to pupils, parents, and advisors is greatly facilitated. Availability, rapidity, accuracy, and extent of analysis possible are the principal overall advantages of data processing in relation to the guidance program.

5. Regular evaluative research must identify and eliminate unnecessary testing and other habitual practices characteristic of overemphasis on testing for its own sake without relation to its instructional use.

6. The major part of our present follow-up effort deals only with those students who plan to attend college. The new design recognizes the need for achieving equivalent service analysis for the noncollege student as well.

7. The Carnegie unit system of grade points and credits continues to be a powerful influence against the achievement of individualism in our schools. The new design recognizes other tools of greater utility to take the place of the Carnegie system. Its elimination will facilitate the adoption of a flexible curriculum which the guidance services of the new design is fashioned to support.

Summary of Advantages Predicted
for the Guidance Program of the New Design

1. It will provide a functional plan for protecting the individuality of students and teachers in an increasingly specialized, potentially bureaucratic school program. It will fix responsibility for continuous educational, vocational, and personal advisement of individual students, responsibility seen to be necessary if the potential values of the new design are to be realized.

2. It will establish a proper relationship between the pupil personnel services department and the instructional departments, and will clearly limit guidance responsibilities to responsibilities belonging properly to the school. School guidance services will become functional in curriculum planning and evaluation, contributing to curriculum innovations which build on individual talents.

3. It will clarify the role of the counseling specialist and provide a basis for proper evaluation of his services to the teaching staff. It will relieve him of difficult, divergent expectations, largely unrealizable. Role expectations of faculty and counseling specialists will converge and reinforce rather than compete. Advisement functions will be more realistically apportioned. Only those problems of advisement requiring extraordinary consideration will be handled by counselors. Routine advisement will be handled by advisement teams, and much of the individual course determination will be based upon individual teacher recommendations.

4. Unnecessary duplication of pupil records and misuse of or failure to use instruments of value in identifying student talents and achievement will be discouraged. Useful personnel information, in usable form, will be made easily accessible to teachers and subject-matter departments when needed. Educational engineering to utilize machine data processing can be instituted and efficiently controlled.

5. Specialists in the various subject-matter fields will become increasingly aware of the interrelationships of their specialty with other departments of instruction as they become more personally involved in academic advisement. Communication between departments seeking better integration of services to the individual student will be encouraged. But subject specialists will *not* be expected to provide instruction in guidance as a part of advisement.

6. The new design recognizes the importance of building students' competence to accumulate and use wisely their own records of achievement. It provides a location for these records and fixes responsibility for their use.

7. The advisement team has advantages of:

   a. Continuity of advisement even with staff turnover.

   b. Leadership in group and individual advisement by the entire academic staff.

   c. Separation of the academic advisement function from the general counseling function of the specialist guidance staff. The concept of "teacher-counselor" is opposed; that of "teacher-advisor" is endorsed.

   d. Flexibility with respect to subgroups (e.g., division of the sexes or grades for special meetings).

8. An instructional component of the guidance program is clearly delineated, substantially strengthening its impact on each student.

The important question, however, still remains. How does this differ from traditional guidance programs and organizations? For example, the new design for guidance may bear a superficial resemblance to the homeroom proposals of several decades ago. One major distinction, obviously, is the fact that the proposed structure offers a framework for differentiated functions and a differentiated staff to cope with specific aspects of the program. The advisement teams are not teacher-counselors. They are basically academic advisors responsible for the soundness of the academic choices made by individual students who do not have unique problems requiring additional professional counsel. The advisement team gains rapport with family and becomes the point of routine contact between the parents and the school. Whenever any special problems develop, the professional guidance staff is immediately called in to assist; or, if it is a persistent or endemic problem, the guidance staff will assume the full advisement responsibility. The concept of the teacher-counselor is completely eliminated as it represents in reality a hybrid without sufficient training or understanding for the problems entailed. Another distinction is the proposal to make instruction in guidance a part of the regular academic curriculum taught by the guidance staff. This recognizes the necessity of making guidance an integral part of the total secondary school program.

The details of any one guidance program have not been outlined in order to retain the flexibility and broad applicability inherent in the entire new design for education. The basic proposition remains that the new design offers a structure—a framework for individualization—without imposing a new orthodoxy in place of the old. The essential common framework of the guidance program involves a functional distinction between advisement teams and counselors, and the establishment of an instructional curriculum in guidance.

8

FIRST STEPS IN
FLEXIBLE SCHEDULING

Before it is appropriate to consider how flexible scheduling can assist the school program, this question must be asked: What is to be accomplished? Do you want to do what you are now doing, *but better,* or do you want to do something different? And, if you want to do something different, what exactly do you anticipate will be facilitated? Often these two elements become confused. Schedule modification implies change, but that change need not be a change in objectives, or even procedures; it may mean only a more efficient implementation of current patterns. In this latter situation, schedule modification points explicitly toward a higher yield,[1] a yield gained almost invariably without the use of additional resources.

Where schedule modification is contemplated in order to alter objectives or procedures, there are three major sources of concern: (1) the lack of resources for change; or (2) the availability of resources but the fear that change will lead to less effective use of resources and hence to a greater and unreasonable demand for even further resources; or (3) the fear that changes will result in violations of law, or tradition.

---

[1] "Yield" here means the efficiency of learning within a given course in a given time or the opportunity to extend the courses taken and topics encountered.

The questions to consider in contemplating schedule modification are these: (1) Given certain resources, how can the most effective program be constructed? (2) What kind of instructional program is the most effective and what resources are needed to implement it?

In Chapter 3, a modular approach to flexible scheduling is presented, an approach which attempts to use any given level of resources to best advantage and to suggest the efficient use of additional resources. What kinds of schedule modification may be implemented short of a total modular approach to the schedule? Scheduling for flexibility may involve only rearrangement of time allotments and sequences of established courses. Other kinds of modification may require schedule preplanning and in still other instances, facility modification is necessary.

It should be emphasized that the various modifications proposed here are not necessarily being advocated, nor are the examples to follow complete. Other modifications and examples could have been given. The intention here is to provide some concrete suggestions of modifications in scheduling which, in various combinations, have given satisfaction in a large number of school situations. By examining the range of possible schedule modifications, an individual school may discover and appraise some new schedule patterns which might facilitate its unique program. Or perhaps a particular type of schedule modification, while not providing an adequate base for actual trial of the full range of variables with which a school wishes to experiment, may prove to be the best possible immediate experience essential for commitment to a broader program modification. Results obtained under such partial implementation require interpretation which recognizes the influence of variables which might not be present if a full program were being implemented. Examples of such variables are balancing staff load, undue complexity, excessive rigidity, and staff satisfaction.

Modifications Requiring Only an Administrative Decision

For purposes of comparison, consider a standard schedule of six classes per day, each of approximately fifty to fifty-five minutes, the same schedule being offered each day. Figure 8.1 is a diagrammatic representation of such a schedule, modeling the most popular current practice in our secondary school.

The simplest modification of this basic pattern involves even period exchange (see Figure 8.2). The only requirement for even period exchange is that an administrative decision be made designating when each period will meet. It might be designated that on Monday, for example, first period will meet during the time normally allocated for first and second periods, and that the second period meeting will be omitted. On Tuesday, the fourth period is omitted and the third period is allocated an additional meeting. This pattern is repeated throughout the week with the result that each class has one extended meeting, but in exchange for this, each class forfeits a fifth meeting weekly. Advantages of this pattern include

FIGURE 8.1. STANDARD SCHEDULE

Period	M	T	W	Th	F
1	1°	1	1	1	1
2	2	2	2	2	2
3	3	3	3	3	3
4	4	4	4	4	4
5	5	5	5	5	5
6	6	6	6	6	6

° Numbers in period blocks refer to class meeting patterns.

FIGURE 8.2. EVEN PERIOD EXCHANGE

Period	M	T	W	Th	F
1	1°	1	1	1	2
2	1	2	2	2	2
3	3	3	3	4	3
4	4	3	4	4	4
5	5	5	6	5	5
6	6	6	6	6	5

° Numbers in period blocks refer to class meeting patterns.

the availability of a longer period of instruction, particularly desirable in some laboratory phases of a course. The chief disadvantage, as compared with the standard schedule, is the forfeiture of daily meeting periods and the rigidity of an imposed common pattern for all subjects, regardless of their instructional requirements, meeting during a given period.

Another modification requiring only administrative decision is block scheduling. See Figures 8.3 and 8.4. In block scheduling, the subjects normally occupying the time for periods 1 and 2 alternate the use of this time daily, period 1 being allocated the entire block of time on Monday, Wednesday, and Friday, and period 2 being allocated the entire block of time on Tuesday and Thursday. In some applications of this pattern, the two periods exchange the time allocated each week. If, during the first week, first period were allocated a double block Monday, Wednesday, and Friday, during the following week, second period would be allocated that amount of time for Monday, Wednesday, and Friday, the first period meeting Tuesday and Thursday.

Block Scheduling

FIGURE 8.3. STRAIGHT BLOCK

Period	M	T	W	Th	F
1	1°	2	1	2	1
2	1	2	1	2	1

° Numbers in period blocks refer to class meeting patterns.

FIGURE 8.4. MODIFIED BLOCK

Period	M	T	W	Th	F°
1	1	2	1	2	1
2	1	2	1	2	2

° Any day could be substituted for Friday for modification.

In other applications, the same meeting pattern is retained for an entire semester, the exchange of the amount of time allocation for first and second periods being reversed during the spring semester. The advantages of this type of scheduling lie principally in the increased length of instructional time, and the disadvantages center around the lack of a daily meeting. This lack becomes especially troublesome in an application where the Tuesday-Thursday meeting pattern results in too much of a break in subject-matter continuity, particularly when a student happens to be absent for one day, say, a Thursday. His absence would result in his not meeting that subject for an entire week—from one Tuesday until the next. Figure 8.4 illustrates a modification in block scheduling which tends to overcome part of this difficulty in that it obviates the need for alternate-week or alternate-semester scheduling by dividing the time on Friday (or any one day per week) as under a conventional schedule, thus giving each subject three meeting days a week.

Another possibility involves period addition (see Figure 8.5). Period addition is a means of providing for different lengths of periods without sacrificing a daily meeting. It is accomplished by

FIGURE 8.5. PERIOD ADDITION

Period	M	T	W	Th	F
1	1*	1	1	1	1
2	2	2	2	2	2

a

Period	M	T	W	Th	F
1	1	1	1	1	1
2	2	2	2	2	2

b

Period	M	T	W	Th	F
1	1	1	1	1	1
x					
2	2	2	2	2	2

c

* Numbers in period blocks refer to class meeting patterns.

designating a part of each period with a special X period to be divided between the two periods on an alternating basis. Periods may be shortened to accommodate the X period with the same total time, or the X period may be of the same or different length. Figure 8.5a shows the original period arrangement; Figure 8.5b illustrates the amount of time which is listed out of the schedule for rearrangement, as shown in 8.5c. Advantages of period addition, again, are primarily to allow for varying the length of instruction without sacrificing a daily meeting. The disadvantages of rigidity, as noted in earlier patterns, still pertain; and of course this and other patterns involving variation in the length of instruction make the assumption that different types of instructional activities appropriately demand different lengths of instructional time.[1]

This particular pattern of schedule modification has most often been applied in the junior high school, in such subjects as music and art. In such cases music meets in the short part of the altered period of instruction, and art in the longer part of the altered period, thus enabling the two courses, normally of only semester length, to be offered over the entire year.

Some schedule patterns, involving only administrative decision to implement, are based on variations and rotation. The simplest of these, involving sequence rotation, is presented in Figure 8.6a. Here the standard pattern is retained in terms of a daily meeting and in terms of length of meeting. The only variation comes from the fact that the rotation of periods changes from day to day. As noted, on Monday, the rotation of periods is the same as for the standard schedule. On Tuesday, the second period comes at the beginning of the day, followed by third period, fourth, fifth, first, and sixth, in that order. It should be noted that sixth period can also be included in the rotation of periods; but in a number of applications, sixth period has been excluded from the rotation because of the requirements in the physical education program.

The advantages of sequence rotation come primarily from the

[1] See Chapter 2.

sharing by all classes of all the minor irritations and interruptions of classroom instruction, e.g., students who are chronically late the beginning of the day, hunger pains that accompany the period just before lunch, all school assemblies, sleepiness that follows lunch, and the restlessness of the last period of the day. This rotation also enables teachers to share different hours of preparation times. Cited disadvantages are the undue complexity of the schedule and the difficulty of being able to keep this schedule straight in terms of what day meets what period at what time. The latter drawback is mostly theoretical in that students and teachers who are working intimately with the scheduling pattern find no difficulty in keeping the meeting times coordinate. Persons having less direct contact with the schedule, such as supporting staff, often do find the adjustment more difficult.

The example of sequence rotation is a rather obvious instance of one possible variation being shown; many other possibilities exist. As indicated, sixth period could be included in a sequence rotation. Other patterns of rotation are also possible. For example, if a block schedule were also in use at the school, it might be desirable to rotate the sequence in a series of two, periods 1 and 2, 3 and 4, and 5 and 6 always being locked together and rotated as a unit.

Displaced rotation is another variety of rotation pattern and scheduling (see Figure 8.6b). Displaced rotation is a means of scheduling a seventh period within the total time allocation of the standard six-period schedule. Under this system, one period a week of each of the other subjects is replaced by instruction in a seventh subject. The advantage is the provision for an additional period of instruction; the disadvantage is that instruction is reduced to four periods a week. Note the two x periods. In some schedules these are used for special events on Friday, or early Friday dismissal; so they are shown as fifth and sixth period on Friday. These x periods can be inserted at any point as needed in the schedule at the discretion of the administrator. It must be pointed out that there is very little evidence to suggest that daily instruction in every subject

FIGURE 8.6. VARIATIONS IN ROTATION

Sequence rotation

Period	M	T	W	Th	F
1	1	2	3	4	5
2	2	3	4	5	1
3	3	4	5	1	2
4	4	5	1	2	3
5	5	1	2	3	4
6	6	6	6	6	6

a

Displaced rotation

Period	M	T	W	Th	F
1	1	7_A	1	1	1
2	2	2	7_B	2	2
3	3	3	3	7_C	3
4	4	4	4	4	7_D
5	5	5	5	5	x
6	6	6	6	6	x

b

is superior to instruction on a less regular basis. Available evidence suggests that the critical nature of daily instruction varies widely with the subject, and although some teachers involved in nondaily instruction feel very strongly that this is not as successful as daily exposure, the tested results have not borne out their assertions.

Period	M	T	W	Th	F
1	1	6	5	4	3
2	2	1	6	5	4
3	3	2	1	6	5
4	4	3	2	1	6
5	5	4	3	2	x

Compressed rotation

c

Period	M	T	W	Th	F
1	1	1	1	1	1
2	1	2	2	2	2
3	2	2	3	3	3
4	3	3	3	4	4
5	4	4	4	4	5
6	5	5	5	5	5
7	6	6	6	6	6

Expanded rotation

d

Another possibility is to take the two periods designated as x periods and provide for additional instruction in any of the seven subjects. This can be done either on a regular basis (for example, fifth and sixth periods each week could *always* have five periods of instruction) or on a rotating basis.

For compressed rotation, see Figure 8.6c. Under the compressed rotation system, five periods are scheduled into the time normally allocated for six. This means that every instructional period is lengthened, but the corresponding difficulty is that daily instruction is sacrificed. Classes offered each day vary. A six-period program is still being offered, although only five of these periods meet on any given day. This rotation pattern results in an x period (shown here as fifth period on Friday afternoon) which can be inserted at any time in the weekly schedule. The chief advantage is an even extension of the length of instruction time; the disadvantage is the forfeiture of a daily instruction period.

In expanded rotation (see Figure 8.6d), the amount of time normally allocated to six periods under the standard schedule is divided into seven periods. By combining the idea of a displaced period with the added period in the schedule, it is possible to have one lengthened period each week. For example, first period meets for first and second periods on Monday and still does not forfeit a daily meeting. Except for this double period, other meetings of a particular class are somewhat shortened. Daily meetings are retained with a provision for varying instructional length, without extending the school day or altering the basic framework. This same scheme also adapts to a straightforward seven-period day. None of the patterns of modification illustrated so far require additional resources, either in facilities or in staff.

With variable period length (see Figure 8.7a) it is also possible to vary the amount of time designated for each period. In the example illustrated, periods 1 and 2 meet for thirty minutes, periods 3 and 4 for fifty minutes, and periods 5 and 6 for seventy minutes. The specific length of time in the periods can be varied to suit the individual application. By itself, this modification is not too feasible, for it permits no variation in time for different phases of a particular course. It combines rigidity with small gains in flexibility for unique courses.

Combining the variable period length with a sequence rotation (as indicated in 8.7b) obviates this difficulty. Each period now has

FIGURE 8.7. VARIABLE PERIOD LENGTH

	M	T	W	Th	F
30	1	1	1	1	1
30	2	2	2	2	2
50	3	3	3	3	3
50	4	4	4	4	4
70	5	5	5	5	5
70	6	6	6	6	6

a

	M	T	W	Th	F
30	1	2	3	4	5
30	2	3	4	5	6
50	3	4	5	6	1
50	4	5	6	1	2
70	5	6	1	2	3
70	6	1	2	3	4

b

some short, some medium, and some long periods, adaptable to varying time requirements of different phases of the course. It can be pointed out that only one or two periods may meet for a non-standard length of time each week, either shorter or longer. All periods need not vary. These lengthened or shortened periods may be rotated to provide for optimal adaptation to instructional purposes and methods.

When considered systematically, a wide number of possibilities can be suggested which involve only administrative decisions for their implementation. None of the patterns proposed in this section involve any additional resources in themselves, although their full implementation can often be facilitated by making additional resources available, as is the case with many kinds of program modifications which do not involve schedule changes.

The various scheduling patterns described so far illustrate well the kinds of alternatives available within rigorous limits of habitual time schedules regardless of whether or not any one of them, followed by inquiry as to their possible value, should be part of initial efforts to introduce flexibility. As faculties become interested in these kinds of change and, through experience, lose uncritical dependence on and blind allegiance to the standard school day of six 55-minute periods, doors open for many more complex possibilities inherent in the new design for secondary education.

Administrative leadership as a first step can encourage departmental specialists to integrate very simple schedule adjustments with planning for team teaching, for more suitable student groupings, and for more efficient and effective types of instruction. Global innovations, which may be ultimately worthwhile, can often best be achieved gradually. High personal costs, associated with such rapid imposition of global change that understanding and confidence of participants fail, may well destroy a creative change before its fruits can ripen.

Other Schedule Modifications

Once a faculty has become familiar with possible variations involving only manipulations of time, thus freeing themselves from dependence on the same egg crate to house all courses, many additional schedule modifications of possible value will appear on the planning horizon. These innovations may integrate combinations of two, three, or all four kinds of decisions.

1. Administrative
2. Schedule preplanning
3. Facility modification
4. Staff changes

Combining Administrative Decision
with Schedule Preplanning

An interesting example of this heading combines period addition with an art-music combination (see Figure 8.8). Here period 1 is three long periods of art and two of music weekly. Period 2 is two extended art periods and three shorter music sessions. The time distribution can be reversed weekly or by semesters. Other course combinations can achieve flexibility in this way: physical education and industrial arts, typing and bookkeeping, home economics and reading laboratory, etc.

FIGURE 8.8. COMBINING PERIOD ADDITION
WITH INTEGRATION OF TWO SUBJECTS

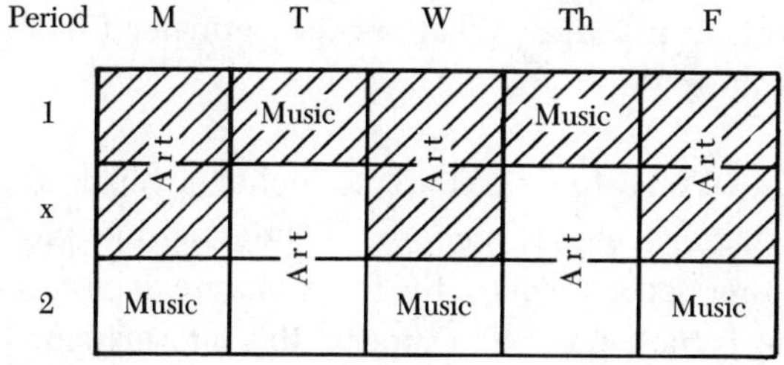

Facility Modification

School faculties are familiar with many facility modifications already accepted in different subject-matter areas, such as shops, language laboratories, home economics, arts and crafts, business education, physical education, and science laboratories. Various kinds of libraries, auditoriums, and multipurpose rooms can be seen in operation throughout the country, most, however, being used with traditional-schedule rigidity.

As ideas of the new design become operative, additional facility modification will frequently be either necessarily prerequisite or highly desirable for competent practice to occur. Decisions as to what facilities to change involve consideration of these major questions:

1. Can various curricular requirements be met through provision of multipurpose facilities easily adaptable to several different functions and methods? Or will multipurpose design destroy the necessary level of competent practice and become, in fact, a waste of money? Guidelines for such choices may well be found in industrial practice, in hospitals, and in other institutions housing a variety of highly specialized workers and services.

2. What alternatives exist in design possibilities for periodic modification to take care of inevitable change in educational practice? What are the predicted possible changes? What are the predicted costs of modifying a facility to accommodate new developments in practice? What are the permanent facilities? The temporary ones? Why?

3. Which functions are so highly specialized and individualized that discrete instructional facilities must be provided, not usable by other departments, if the functions are to be accomplished at all? What is the evidence to support this information?

In order for school leadership to make such decisions, essential resource data will be necessary (1) to evaluate adaptability of facilities, (2) to determine obsolescence in present housing and equipment, (3) to identify the functions of various special-purpose, noninstructional spaces such as teacher offices for team conferences, (4) to determine the physical location of various spaces in relation to each other, (5) to estimate the costs of construction and maintenance, and (6) to assess the extent of utilization of present and proposed facilities.

Senior teachers should participate in making these decisions. Failure to involve them as resource people in answering questions relating to their own area of expert practice has been all too often an expensive mistake. Properly planned facilities add to flexibility without denying special functions and methods.

As master teachers and architects plan facility modification, these essential steps are most important:

1. The definition and purpose of the facility must be established. Is it a laboratory? A large-group instructional area? A small-group area? A research or reference area? An individual study area? An auditorium?

2. What size groups must it serve? How often?

3. What kind of instructional methodology will occur in it?

4. What specific equipment does competent practice of this methodology require?

Figure 8.9 illustrates this sequence applied to laboratory facilities. Similar considerations apply to planning for large-group, small-group, and individual areas of instruction. These latter facilities generally can be designed to provide greater flexibility of use by different departments than is true of laboratories. Individual study cubicles, small-group discussion areas, libraries, conference rooms,

FIGURE 8.9. PLANNING PHYSICAL FACILITIES FOR LABORATORIES

1. Definition and Purposes:

   Laboratory as here defined includes those physical facilities provided where specific equipment and tools are needed to enable students to work independently and in small groups to practice skills, to experiment, and to apply ideas suggested in large-group instruction.

2. Kinds and Sizes of Laboratories (examples):

   a. Experimental science labs—45 students
   b. Foreign language labs—45 students
   c. Reading and study skill labs—30 students
   d. Math labs—60 students
   e. Art labs, craft labs, shops—60 students
   f. Libraries—150 students
   g. Social science labs—75 students
   h. Office machines centers—60 students
   i. Playing fields and gyms—45 to 150 students
   j. Instructional materials production
      center—15 students

3. Types of Laboratories:

   Experimental
   Drill
   Application
   Research

4. Physical Facilities:

   Unique for each type of laboratory

and large lecture halls can be equipped to serve most subject-matter areas interchangeably.

Scheduling of large-group areas, small-group areas, and individual study spaces which adapt to cross-departmental use offers many interesting possibilities. These combine, in various ways, two basic concepts of facility scheduling: (1) horizontal scheduling and (2) vertical scheduling.

Figure 8.10 illustrates horizontal scheduling, showing three possibilities. Course phases and weekly cycles may vary. The requirement is that all sections of one large group of students in a particular course be scheduled in one or two periods of the day.

Figure 8.11 illustrates vertical scheduling, showing distribution of ten sections over six periods.

As schedule planners seek optimal cross-departmental utilization of shared facilities, combination of vertical and horizontal patterns becomes helpful. Figure 8.12 illustrates the possible scheduling of a large auditorium to serve social studies, mathematics, English, science, and one additional department. This arrangement gives each department the auditorium for one period each day, for five days of the week.

FIGURE 8.10. VARIETIES OF HORIZONTAL SCHEDULING OF
300 SOCIAL STUDIES STUDENTS IN TEN SECTIONS

Period	M	T	W	Th	F	
1	10 sections	10 sections	10 sections	10 sections	10 sections	One basic horizontal group of 10 sections
2			or			
3	5 sections	5 sections	5 sections	5 sections	5 sections	Two basic horizontal groups, less conflict
4	5 sections	5 sections	5 sections	5 sections	5 sections	
5			or			
6	8 sections	8 sections	8 sections	8 sections	8 sections	One basic horizontal group of 8 sections plus 2 more in any period to relieve subject conflicts

Note: Weekly cycles may not require five-day-a-week meetings. It is necessary only that sections be scheduled horizontally for a particular period.

FIGURE 8.11. SHOWING VERTICAL SCHEDULING

Period	M	T	W	Th	F
1	Sect. I, II				
2	Sect. III, IV	→			
3	Sect. V, VI	→	Distributed over the week according to designed course cycles		
4	Sect. VII	→			
5	Sect. VIII				
6	Sect. IX, X				

FIGURE 8.12. SCHEDULING A LARGE AUDITORIUM FOR ONE WEEK

Period	M	T	W	Th	F
1	Social studies	English	Math	Science	Other
2	English	Math	Science	Other	Social studies
3	Math	Science	Other	Social studies	English
4	Science	Other	Social studies	English	Math
5	Other	Social studies	English	Math	Science
6	Other	English	Math	Science	Social studies

Figure 8.13 illustrates a pattern for scheduling either small-group areas or individual study spaces which can be integrated either vertically or horizontally with large-group instruction scheduled according to Figure 8.12. This permits either horizontal or vertical offsets adapting small-group and individual study to planned large-group phases in particular departments.

Paired facility utilization can apply to large- and small-group phases of two departments, such as English and social studies, or within a department, such as English alone.

These distributions of space can vary in many different ways. Total space for different kinds of instruction allocated to any one subject-matter area will be a function of the distribution of course phases and their natures which each department designs, and the course cycles which integrate them, as discussed previously in Chapter 3.

FIGURE 8.13. SCHEDULING A SET OF SMALL-GROUP FACILITIES TO INTEGRATE WITH THE ABOVE LARGE-GROUP PATTERN BY HORIZONTAL OR VERTICAL OFFSET (TWENTY STANDARD-SIZE OR FIFTEEN STUDENT-CAPACITY CLASSROOMS)

Period	M	T	W	Th	F
1	Other	Social studies	English	Math	Science
2	Social studies	English	Math	Science	Other
3	English	Math	Science	Other	Social studies
4	Math	Science	Other	Social studies	English
5	Science	Other	Social studies	English	Math
6	Other	Social studies	English	Math	Science

FIGURE 8.14. SHOWING NECESSARY EQUIVALENT EDUCATIONAL AREAS FOR
EACH PHASE OF A PARTICULAR COURSE, HAVING SIMILAR TIME MODULES

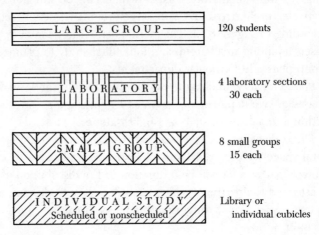

LARGE GROUP — 120 students

LABORATORY — 4 laboratory sections / 30 each

SMALL GROUP — 8 small groups / 15 each

INDIVIDUAL STUDY / Scheduled or nonscheduled — Library or / individual cubicles

Generally, scheduling of facilities modified to serve special purposes and unique course phases cannot be separated from departmental design of phases and staff-utilization decisions. When a particular course includes for all its enrollment the four types of instruction proposed in the new design, total allocation of facilities must match for each phase the distributed large group. This is illustrated by Figure 8.14.

The relationship of course phases in a particular subject-matter grouping and of staff utilization to facility modification planning is further illustrated in Figure 8.15 which shows a possible arrangement for 165 mathematics students assigned to a comprehensive low-interest group. Here are illustrated variations in time modules, group size, and instructional types in one course cycle. Thirty gifted eighth graders and 15 limited eleventh graders meet with the ninth-grade large group. According to variations in abilities and needs, the distribution of students into large laboratories, small-group sections, and short laboratories is seen to be quite flexible. It becomes evident that without facility modification some schools could not implement such a program.

Variations in Class-size Innovations

The simplest class-size innovation brings together, into one large group, two or more traditional classes studying the same subject in the same block of time or period (see Figure 8.16). This process is reversible. A basic large group can be broken up taking some or all students and distributing them into small sections of various sizes appropriate to different course phases (see Figure 8.17). Here

FIGURE 8.15. SHOWING INTERRELATIONSHIP OF FACILITY PLANNING, STAFF UTILIZATION, AND COURSE PHASES FOR A COMPREHENSIVE LOW-INTEREST, NINTH-GRADE MATHEMATICS GROUP

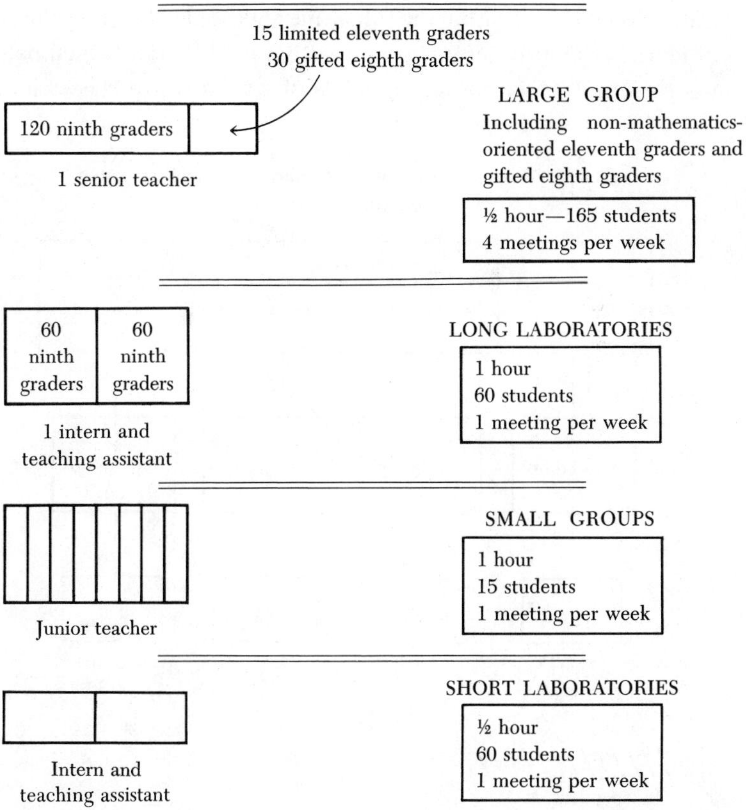

15 limited eleventh graders
30 gifted eighth graders

120 ninth graders

1 senior teacher

LARGE GROUP
Including non-mathematics-oriented eleventh graders and gifted eighth graders

½ hour—165 students
4 meetings per week

60 ninth graders	60 ninth graders

1 intern and teaching assistant

LONG LABORATORIES

1 hour
60 students
1 meeting per week

Junior teacher

SMALL GROUPS

1 hour
15 students
1 meeting per week

Intern and teaching assistant

SHORT LABORATORIES

½ hour
60 students
1 meeting per week

FIGURE 8.16. COMBINING STANDARD-SIZE CLASSES
INTO ONE LARGE BASIC GROUP

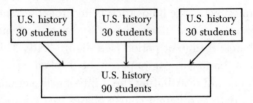

variations in class size can be built around any kind of distribution pattern according to abilities, needs, and interests of subgroups. All, however, must fit into the same time block. They also must adapt to time distributions within the total time allocated to the time block.

Figure 8.18 illustrates a very interesting modification which permits the combination of any number of standard-size classes into

FIGURE 8.17. DISTRIBUTION OF LARGE GROUPS INTO SMALL GROUPS
OF VARIOUS SIZES

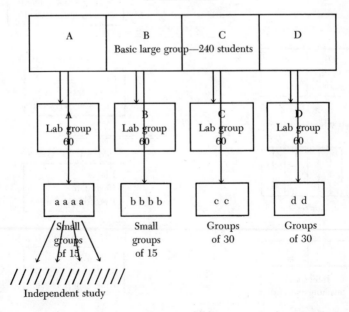

FIGURE 8.18. ELECTRONIC-CLASS COMBINATION

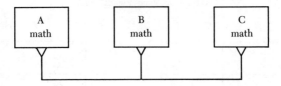

one large group by means of electronic aids. The same expert presentation or demonstration, whether live or on video tape, is conveyed to several classes at the same time. Interestingly, different teachers can contribute effectively to a planned sequence of large-group teaching and learning periods in this way. Aside from the necessary closed-circuit electronic equipment, no special facility modification is necessary. Classes do not have to move for follow-up instruction in standard-size groups. When tapes are used they can be placed in the library where individual students may use them for review and self-directed inquiry. All classes, in any one department or combined departments, can be brought together, by flipping a switch, to participate in a common learning experience. The arrangement can be tied in with live broadcasts, with no local or international geographical limitation. This innovation has the advantage of less movement of students from space to space, immediate feedback and evaluation of large-group presentations through discussion in small-group situations, and it eliminates the need for large instructional spaces.

Horizontal Class Groupings

Another possibly useful grouping within a department is illustrated in Figure 8.19. Here all U.S. history classes are daily scheduled during the first three periods. All social problems classes are scheduled in the fourth, fifth, and sixth periods. Teachers of U.S. history concentrate their major instructional responsibility in this subject in the morning. They are available twice a week in the after-

FIGURE 8.19. SHOWING HORIZONTAL CLASS GROUPING OF U.S. HISTORY
AND SOCIAL PROBLEMS CLASSES

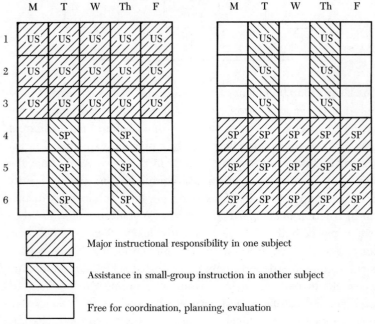

Major instructional responsibility in one subject

Assistance in small-group instruction in another subject

Free for coordination, planning, evaluation

Notes:
1. All U.S. history classes meet periods 1 to 3 each day.
2. All social problems classes meet periods 4 to 6 each day.
3. Teachers have major responsibility for instruction in only one subject.
4. Teachers have assistant responsibility with small groups in a related subject.
5. Each teacher has an afternoon or a morning free for planning, evaluation, and co-ordination three days each week.

noon to assist with social problems groups of 25 students each. Social problems teachers have full responsibility for one subject in the afternoon and assist two days a week with small groups in U.S. history in the morning. By appropriate planning of course phases over the weekly cycle:

> Five teachers, aided by teaching assistants and clerks, can handle 750 U.S. history students in the morning.

Five teachers, aided by teaching assistants and clerks, can handle 750 social problems students in the afternoon.

These ten teachers would be available two days a week for small-group instruction in either the morning or the afternoon. Each teacher would have three afternoons or mornings each week free from instructional responsibilities and available to them for coordination, planning, and evaluation.

Coordinated Intersubject Scheduling

Figure 8.20 illustrates a scheduling innovation involving integration of two subject-matter areas, English and history. Two groups,

FIGURE 8.20. COORDINATED INTERSUBJECT SCHEDULING:
ENGLISH AND HISTORY

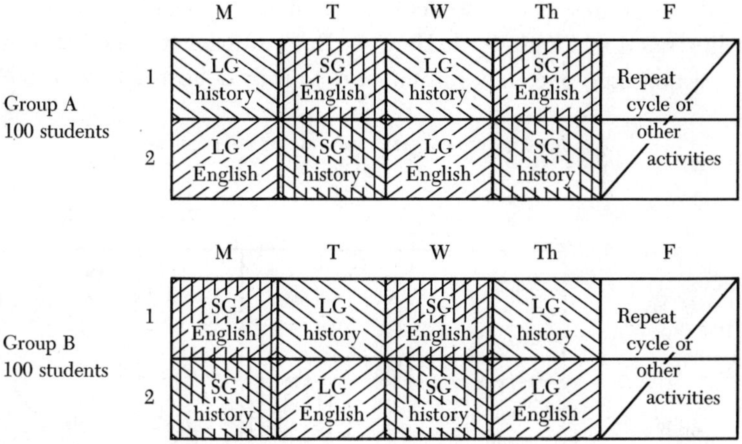

Two groups of 100 each are scheduled into common periods for English and history.
Five small groups of 20 students each are scheduled on alternate days.
Staff requirements:
  First period daily: 1 history teacher, 5 English teachers
  Second period daily: 5 history teachers, 1 English teacher
  For support: 1 teaching assistant, 1 clerk

A and B, are scheduled into common periods for two subjects. Course structures for the two subjects are the same, requiring two large-group meetings and two small-group meetings of equal length each week in each subject. The fifth day of the week may be scheduled for other subjects, independent study, or repetition of the cycle. Staffing of this schedule will require, for first period, five English teachers and one history teacher and, for second period, one English teacher and five history teachers. A total of six teachers, plus a teaching assistant and a clerk, can thus serve 200 students in an integrated program of history and English. Students in the two groups need not be at the same grade level.

Coordinated Intrasubject Scheduling

The modification suggested above may be usefully applied as well to two groups of 100 students each in the same subject. This is illustrated in Figure 8.21. Here six English teachers, one teaching assistant, and one clerk form a team to provide instruction for 200

FIGURE 8.21. COORDINATED INTRASUBJECT SCHEDULING: ENGLISH ONLY

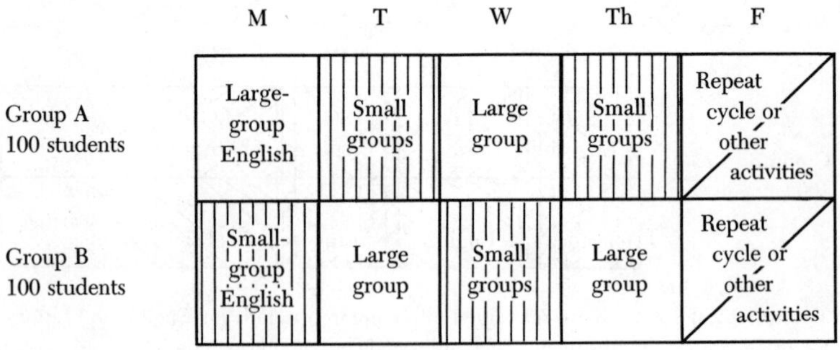

Staff requirements for 200 students:
    6 English teachers
    1 teaching assistant
    1 clerk

students. Facilities to accommodate this innovation include one room, of capacity 100, to house large groups and five small rooms, of capacity 20, to take care of small groups. Advantages recommending this approach to flexibility include optimal use of English facilities, adaptability to different ability groupings of the 200 students, better use of individual teacher talents, and relative simplicity. Departments may find this modification a fruitful start in their exploration of schedule modifications. Students need not be at the same grade level.

Summary of Types of Schedule Modification

The foregoing illustrations by no means exhaust schedule innovation possibilities. Appraisal of them should lead to the realization that flexibility has many dimensions of curriculum time, of instructional modes, of personnel, and of facilities. Planners must keep aware that to achieve flexibility in any dimension requires a price of some other kind of rigidity. Adaptations to free specializations for more effective achievement of group purposes always require new controls and limitations to be operable. Departments and teachers who seek more freedom without consequent responsibilities to other departments and teachers will be disappointed. They should seek both new organizations to improve educational services *and* the necessary new controls to implement these. One without the other cannot be realized.

Figure 8.22 graphically summarizes types of schedule modifications related to typical traditional practice. Integration of one or any combination of these types defines the adventure of the new design. These decision elements highlight the adventure:

1. Decisions on course offerings
2. Decisions on pupil demand
3. Decisions on conflict resolution
4. Decisions on the master schedule

FIGURE 8.22. TYPES OF SCHEDULE MODIFICATION

Variable period length (now one hour is typical).

Variable rotation of classes (now rotation and time are constant).

Variable school year (now two semesters and three months summer holiday).

Variable class size (now thirty students is typical).

Variable grouping of students (now all of any one subject either homogeneous or heterogeneous).

Variable staffing (now one teacher is typical for one course).

PERIOD LENGTH

ROTATION OF CLASSES

SCHOOL YEAR

CLASS SIZE

GROUPING

V A R I A T I O N S

REQUIRED AND ELECTIVE COURSES

NUMBER OF COURSES PER SEMESTER

TIME ALLOCATIONS

COURSE CYCLES

Variable patterns, course cycles (now daily is typical).

Variable total time allocation for each course (now five class hours per week is typical).

Variable number of courses taken in one semester (now five or six per semester is typical).

Variable required subjects in the curriculum (now varies from all requirements in some subjects to none in others).

As groups plan together, the following schedule compromises will contribute to the interesting experience, stimulating both individual creativity and skill in group responsibility:

1. Compromises in class size
2. Facility compromise
3. Grouping compromise
4. Compromise in personnel requirements
5. Adjustments in numbers of sections
6. Adjustments due to student-program changes
7. Change in course offerings
8. Adjustments with traditions
9. Adjustments for experimentation and research
10. Idiosyncratic factors

The new design offers reassurance to school leadership that *responsibly planned schedule innovation* can generate rich rewards in the quest for excellent secondary education. The new design recommends no change for its own sake, recognizing that critical appraisal of many established practices will justify their retention, as alternatives to some new proposals.

9

EXAMPLES OF
THE NEW DESIGN:
PROGRAM AND FACILITIES

Implementation of the assumptions and combination of the many ideas discussed in Chapters 1 through 8 require a substantially different program from that which now exists in most American high schools. These possible program changes are determined to a degree by school size. In this chapter a six-year secondary school enrolling 1,800 students has been postulated, from which specific examples of the new design will be drawn. Three hundred students enrolled at each grade level, 7 through 12, are assumed. As more and more suburban high schools are being built for between 1,500 and 2,000 students, 1,800 may be close to the modal size of secondary schools in the total national picture.

Some Specifications and Definitions

Time and Class-size Modules   In developing a flexible schedule, the basic building blocks for its construction must be determined. District policy must designate the smallest number of students and the shortest period of time that would be used for any instruction. All larger classes and longer class periods must consist of multiples of these basic units or modules, as illustrated in Chapter 3. The modules chosen herein follow:

118

Time module = one-half hour
Class-size module = fifteen students[1]

If a particular school wished, these modules could be shorter or longer, larger or smaller; the school may change its specifications as the need arises. Chapter 3 illustrates these possible variations.

Length of the School Day   District policy establishes the length of the school day even before schedule construction begins. The example here assumes school will be open at 8 A.M. and close at 4 P.M. This gives a *16-period* day based on the time module of ½ hour, or 30 minutes. A 5-day week thus contains 5 × 16 or 80 time modules—½-hour building blocks available for scheduling.

The Course-cycle Module   In most high schools each course structure repeats daily. The example here extends the course cycle to one week of five days. A two-week module, four-week module, or six-week module may prove reasonable under some situations in the future, but as a first departure from a daily cycle, a weekly cycle appears practical. Such a weekly cycle extends the possible variations of schedule-time distribution from an area of 16 time blocks to 80 time blocks.

Allocation of Time in Weekly Schedule Module According to Functions and Purposes Served   In the illustration given here of the 80 periods available, 15 are reserved for necessary activities other than classroom instruction and 5 periods are reserved for guidance teaching. Ten periods have been reserved for faculty meetings, departmental meetings, grade-level meetings, special staff meetings, and similar needs. These 10 periods represent 2 time blocks a day, or an average of one hour daily. Students may be expected to use this time for travel to and from school, or as they may wish for individual study, concentrations in some area of special interest, or for activities.

---

[1] The student module is not rigid. It provides a convenient unit. Uneven multiples on smaller classes are possible.

For lunch, one daily time module has been allowed. The guidance time systematically provides the equivalent of ½ hour daily for guidance instruction. Five periods for guidance plus 10 for meetings plus 5 for lunch equals 20 periods reserved out of the 80 available each week. Sixty periods remain for instruction in the six basic subject-matter fields.

An arbitrary allocation of an average of 20 per cent of the instructional time has been provided for individual study, for the purposes and values described in Chapter 4. Ideally, the proportion of time devoted to this individual study should increase as students progress from the seventh through the twelfth grade, yet the average allocation for each year will be too much or too little, depending on the individual student. Some will use well much more than 20 per cent of unsupervised time; others should have less, and some, none at all. By the time each finishes high school, he should demonstrate his capacity for substantial self-direction.

Figure 9.1 summarizes the above specifications.

A Basic Instructional Framework for the
Six-year High School

Once district policy has defined the foregoing specifications, the basic distribution of instructional time among the six subject-matter areas can proceed grade level by grade level. In Figure 9.1 there are 60 instructional periods available each year, totaling 360 periods over the six-year span. School leadership must decide how to distribute the time among six domains of knowledge. Each area, following the second assumption in Chapter 2, must be studied for a required common minimum of time. Beyond this minimum, each area of subject matter will offer additional study opportunities for individual student concentration. Total time available, then, must be allocated to (1) requirements for all in each subject-matter area, (2) individual study, and (3) concentration for special talents and interests.

FIGURE 9.1. ONE POSSIBILITY OF SPECIFICATIONS AND DEFINITIONS
FOR THE ORGANIZATION OF THE HIGH SCHOOL PROGRAM

1. Six-year high school (grades 7–12)
   300 students at each grade level . . . . 1,800 students
2. Smallest number of students to be scheduled
   for any group in any subject
   (defined as 1 student module) . . . .   15 students
3. Instructional periods to be scheduled
   (classes may be more than one period long) . . . .   30 minutes
4. Length of school day
   (8 A.M. to 4 P.M.) . . . .   16 periods
5. Number of days before schedule repeats itself
   (defined as the schedule cycle). . . . .   5 days
6. Periods reserved for other than classroom
   instruction. . . . .   15 periods
   a. Faculty, departmental, grade-level, and other
      staff meetings (2 periods daily × 5 days).   10
   b. Lunch (1 period × 5 days).   5
                                                                        15 periods
7. Guidance . . . .   5 periods
8. Periods remaining for instruction in subject areas . . . .   60 periods
9. Periods reserved for students' independent study,
   20 per cent (60 × 20 per cent). . . . .   12 periods
10. Net time to be scheduled for classroom
    instruction for each student . . . .   48 periods

Figure 9.2a illustrates the blanks which these decisions will fill.
The right-hand column figures are determined from the specifications in Figure 9.1. The first decision fills the blanks in the bottom
row. This gives the total allocation to each subject-matter area
over the six-year span, the total required time, and the total for
individual study and concentration. This allocation will vary according to the specific high school community; it should not be the
same for rural, urban, and suburban high school situations, and
should be modifiable as evaluation indicates. The allocation is necessary, as departments plan for each grade level, for it sets the limits
within which each must operate. Allocation totals for required
columns should be made before concentration and individual totals
are attempted. Figure 9.2b illustrates one possible solution to the

FIGURE 9.2*a*. BASIC FRAMEWORK—SIX-YEAR HIGH SCHOOL

Grade level	Requirements by each subject area						Requirements at each grade level	Available for concentration	Reserved for individual study	Totals available from Figure 9.1
	Mathematics	Science	Social studies	English and foreign languages	Business education, practical, visual, and performing arts	Physical education				
7	?	?	?	?	?	?	?	?	?	60
8	?	?	?	?	?	?	?	?	?	60
9	?	?	?	?	?	?	?	?	?	60
10	?	?	?	?	?	?	?	?	?	60
11	?	?	?	?	?	?	?	?	?	60
12	?	?	?	?	?	?	?	?	?	60
Total minimum require-ments	?	?	?	?	?	?	?	?	?	←360

Decision 1

To be made by curriculum council and guidance council in accordance with district policy

Decision 2

To be made by subject-matter departments after consultation with grade-level guidance teams. Totals must match decision 1.

Decision 3

Time at each grade level for concentration and individual study. To be made by curriculum council and guidance council. Totals must match decision 1.

FIGURE 9.2*b*. SHOWING COMPLETION OF THE BOTTOM ROW
AS THE FIRST DECISION TO BE MADE

Grade level	Requirements by each subject area						Requirements at each grade level	Available for concentration	Reserved for individual study	Totals available from Figure 9.1
	Mathematics	Science	Social studies	English and foreign languages	Business education, practical, visual, and performing arts	Physical education				
7	?	?	?	?	?	?	?	?	?	60
8	?	?	?	?	?	?	?	?	?	60
9	?	?	?	?	?	?	?	?	?	60
10	?	?	?	?	?	?	?	?	?	60
11	?	?	?	?	?	?	?	?	?	60
12	?	?	?	?	?	?	?	?	?	60
Total minimum requirements	30	30	30	60	30	30	210	78	72	360

Variations in decision 1

Total minimum requirements	20	20	20	40	20	20	140	148	72	360

or

Total minimum requirements	15	15	15	40	110	15	210	78	72	360

All times shown are number of half-hour periods per week required.

first decision. This assigns to each department of study, including foreign languages, a total of 30 periods of required instruction each year over the six-year span: $7 \times 30 = 210$ periods of required courses; $360 - 210 = 150$ periods remaining for allocation to individual study and concentration. According to specifications in Figure 9.1, 20 per cent of the 360 periods for instruction must be allocated to individual study: $0.20 \times 360 = 72$ periods. Subtracting this from 150 gives 78 periods left for concentration, thus completing decision 1.

Certainly some schools should not follow the required allocation proposed here. In communities where a large percentage of high school graduates must seek and qualify for self-supporting employment, larger amounts of time for business education and practical arts may well be desirable, with a decrease in required time for foreign language and English, or a decrease distributed over the other departments. Other communities may wish to decrease required time and allow more time for elective concentration adapted to individual interests and talents.

Once the total time assigned to each department is determined, the next decision distributes this time over the six grade levels. Departmental specialists define objectives for required courses at each grade, design course structure to achieve these objectives, assess minimum time necessary to achieve them well, and then decide predicted optimal time allotments for each grade. The sum of these must equal the total time allocated to the department. Each department must keep in mind that these times are minimal requirements, and each will plan additional time for concentration and perhaps individual study as elected by individual students. Grade-level guidance teachers can make valuable decisions in this area. Figure 9.2c illustrates one possible answer to these decisions which complete the columns under "Requirements by each subject area." Note that with the exception of social studies, required time decreases as students progress toward high school graduation. The trend is clearly shown in the seventh column.

FIGURE 9.2c. SHOWING COMPLETION OF COLUMNS UNDER REQUIREMENTS
FOR EACH SUBJECT-MATTER AREA AS THE SECOND DECISION TO BE MADE

Grade level	Requirements by each subject area						Requirements at each grade level	Available for concentration	Reserved for individual study	Totals available from Figure 9.1
	Mathematics	Science	Social studies	English and foreign languages	Business education, practical, visual, and performing arts	Physical education				
7	7	5	5	12	8	7	44	?	?	60
8	7	5	5	12	6	6	41	?	?	60
9	5	7	5	10	5	5	38	?	?	60
10	5	5	5	10	5	5	34	?	?	60
11	3	5	5	8	3	3	28	?	?	60
12	3	3	5	8	3	3	25	?	?	60
Total minimum require-ments	30	30	30	60	30	30	210	78	72	360

All times shown are number of half-hour periods per week required.

The difference between total required time and 60 periods at each grade level gives the half-hour periods available weekly for concentration and individual study. Decisions as to how much time to allocate to each function represent the final step in completing the six-year framework. These decisions should involve the curriculum council and the grade-level advisement team. Information necessary to make them includes careful definition of concentration purposes and course phases, predicted student needs and selections, accurate student personnel information, and good interdepartment communications; of course facilities available add to the possible limitations here. Totals must balance vertically and horizontally. Figure 9.2d completes the basic framework which then sets necessary limits to departmental planning of the time variations in course structures.

FIGURE 9.2d. SHOWING ONE POSSIBLE BASIC FRAMEWORK DECISION

| Grade level | Requirements by each subject area | | | | | | Requirements at each grade level | Available for concentration | Reserved for individual study | Totals available from Figure 9.1 |
	Mathematics	Science	Social studies	English and foreign languages	Business education, practical, visual, and performing arts	Physical education				
7	7	5	5	12	8	7	44	8	8	60
8	7	5	5	12	6	6	41	9	10	60
9	5	7	5	10	5	5	38	10	12	60
10	5	5	5	10	5	5	34	14	12	60
11	3	5	5	8	3	3	28	18	14	60
12	3	3	5	8	3	3	25	19	16	60
Total minimum requirements	30	30	30	60	30	30	210	78	72	360

All times shown are number of half-hour periods per week required.

Designing the Instructional Framework
for Individual Subject Areas

Once the curricular framework described above has been defined, the various subject-matter departments can develop the individual curricula to fit the total pattern. To that end (1) aims must be identified for each grade level and for each group of students at that grade; (2) the scope and sequence must be determined—what content should be included at each grade level, for each group, in each course; (3) departments must establish minimum requirements related to basic aims for each course at each grade level; and (4) decisions must be made as to course structure for each group planned for, the phases, time allocations, sizes of groups, facilities and staff needed, and types of instruction involved. Some of these things, of course, have been done as the overall framework decisions were developed. Each department now adjusts its preliminary planning to the overall pattern allocated to it. Examples for selected departments follow.

Defining Departmental Aims

Departments are encouraged to develop aims related to the kinds of student groupings (shown in Figure 9.3a) which they plan to use. Departments will vary in grouping students, some forming but two basic groups—comprehensive and gifted—others planning for six or seven—limited ability, remedial, gifted, and others. Grouping decisions evolve from relating the subject-matter goals to predicted compositions of student bodies.

A sample statement of aims for mathematics instruction follows:

> I. *Comprehensive group*
>> A. Low interest
>>> 1. Basic skill maintenance

2. Development and maintenance of general skills and concepts
3. General application of skills and concepts
4. Ability and disposition to go beyond present knowledge
5. Historical and cultural perspective of mathematics

B. High interest

1. Basic skill maintenance
2. Development and maintenance of general skills and concepts
3. General application of skills and concepts
4. Ability and disposition to go beyond present knowledge
5. Development of special technical skills
6. Technical application of skills and concepts
7. Historical and cultural perspective of mathematics

II. *Subject-talented*

A. Low interest

1. Advanced skill maintenance and concept development
2. Historical and cultural perspective of mathematics
3. Application of advanced skills and concepts
4. Ability and disposition to go beyond present knowledge

B. High interest

1. Advanced skill maintenance and concept development
2. Historical and cultural perspective of mathematics

3. Application of advanced skills and concepts
4. Ability and disposition to go beyond present knowledge
5. Development of advanced technical skills and concepts
6. Application of technical skills and concepts to basic operations in technical fields
7. Application of mathematical skills to research in technical fields

III. *Special groups*

   A. Remedial (in addition to regular group placement)

      1. Overcome disabilities in mathematics
      2. Simple skill and concept development and maintenance
      3. Appreciation of value of mathematics
      4. Assignment to appropriate group

   B. Limited potential

      1. Development and maintenance of simple concepts and skills
      2. Appreciation of value of mathematics
      3. Limited application of mathematical skills

   C. Mathematics-gifted (to be provided for on an individual basis)

      1. Advanced skill maintenance and concept development
      2. Historical and cultural perspective of mathematics
      3. Application of advanced skills and concepts
      4. Ability and disposition to go beyond present knowledge
      5. Development of advanced technical skills and concepts

6. Application of technical skills and concepts to basic operations in technical fields
7. Application of mathematical skills to research in technical fields
8. Development of independence in mathematical investigation
9. Development of specialized talents

This mathematics department has planned for seven groups at each grade level, indicating a highly diversified program. Such diversification may well be less appropriate in other departments of the same school. Also conceivable is even greater diversification.

Designing a Basic Framework for a Specific Department

Having defined aims and determined groupings of students, individual departments, within the time allocation decisions (Figure 9.2*a*), now proceed to develop a basic framework of their own, a framework which indicates the time for basic requirements and additional concentrations reserved for each instructional group at each grade level for the predicted number of students.

Figure 9.3*a* illustrates one such framework for guiding these decisions in a mathematics department. In its final form this framework must be consistent, in total time allocations for basic requirements, with the departmental allocations agreed upon in Figure 9.2*c*. The department has decided to provide for six groupings of students at each grade level. As indicated in Figure 9.1, all groups are required to take thirty periods of mathematics per week. It was decided to reduce this to eighteen for the limited group. Students assigned to remedial periods are already in the basic group. A single concentration of twelve periods is planned for groups II and III, a double concentration of twenty-four periods for group IV, and a single concentration for students needing remedial instruction. Group I and group V have no additional concentration periods. These decisions are indicated in the additional concentration row of Figure 9.3a.

The mathematics department must now decide how best to distribute available periods of instruction for each group over the six-year span and must estimate the number of students to plan for in each year. These decisions complete the framework as shown in Figure 9.3b. Most departments will find it desirable to start with the basic group (since this group needs no additional concentrations of study time) and build additional concentration periods on this for the other groups. In the example given it should be noted that the required time for basic studies in mathematics starts with seven periods a week for the seventh and eighth grades, drops to five periods weekly for the ninth and tenth grades and three periods each for the eleventh and twelfth. Some subject-matter areas may reverse this, increasing basic requirements from year to year. Because mathematics is a tool for a variety of later pursuits, it is important to concentrate required time in the early grades. This pattern of decreasing amount of instruction as the student proceeds through high school prevails for all mathematics groups, as additional concentrations are added, except for group IV—subject-talented high interest. With this group additional time is concentrated in the ninth, tenth, and eleventh grades.

Group V, students identified as limited in mathematics ability, is not required to meet the basic requirements of group I. A basic study program of three periods per week distributed over the six-year span is planned for them. Some may argue that these students are the very ones who should spend more time than the others on

FIGURE 9.3a. FRAMEWORK FOR DESIGNING MATHEMATICS DEPARTMENT CURRICULUM STRUCTURE SHOWING FIRST TWO DEPARTMENTAL DECISIONS

GROUPS TO BE PROVIDED FOR

Grade level	I Comprehensive low-interest basic group		II Comprehensive high interest		III Subj.-talented low interest		IV Subj.-talented high interest		V Limited		VI Remedial	
	No. of per.	No. of stud.	No. of per.	No. of stud.	No. of per.	No. of stud.	No. of per.	No. of stud.	No. of per.	No. of stud.	No. of per.	No. of stud.
Total periods basic requirement	30	xx	30	xx	30	xx	30	xx	18	xx	0	xx
Additional concentration	0	?	12	?	12	?	24	?	0	?	12	xx
7	?	?	?	?	?	?	?	?	?	?	?	?
8	?	?	?	?	?	?	?	?	?	?	?	?
9	?	?	?	?	?	?	?	?	?	?	?	?
10	?	?	?	?	?	?	?	?	?	?	?	?
11	?	?	?	?	?	?	?	?	?	?	?	?
12	?	?	?	?	?	?	?	?	?	?	?	?
Total periods scheduled	30	xx	42	xx	42	xx	54	xx	18	xx	12	xx
Av. no. students	xx	?	xx	?	xx	?	xx	?	xx	?	xx	?

Decision 1

Decision 2

Decision 3

Determined by Figure 9.2b—note variation for group V (Limited)

Departmental decision as to which groups should have additional concentrations and for how many periods

Departmental decisions distributing available periods of instruction by grade level for each group and estimating number of students to provide for in each group

Departmental decision as to what groups of students should be planned for to best achieve mathematics objectives

132

FIGURE 9.3b. A COMPLETED FRAMEWORK FOR MATHEMATICS DEPARTMENT CURRICULUM STRUCTURE

Grade level	GROUPS TO BE PROVIDED FOR											
	I Comprehensive low-interest basic group		II Comprehensive high interest		III Subj.-talented low interest		IV Subj.-talented high interest		V Limited		VI Remedial	
	No. of per.	No. of stud.	No. of per.	No. of stud.	No. of per.	No. of stud.	No. of per.	No. of stud.	No. of per.	No. of stud.	No. of per.	No. of stud.
Total periods basic requirement	30	xx	30	xx	30	xx	30	xx	18	xx	0	xx
Additional concentration	0	xx	12	xx	12	xx	24	xx	0	xx	12	xx
7	7	120	7	30	8	105	8	30	3	15	5	30
8	7	120	7	30	8	105	8	30	3	15	4	20
9	5	105	8	30	7	105	10	45	3	15	2	15
10	5	105	8	30	7	105	10	45	3	15	1	10
11	3	105	6	30	6	105	10	45	3	15		
12	3	105	6	30	6	105	8	45	3	15		
Total periods scheduled	30	xx	42	xx	42	xx	54	xx	18	xx	12	xx
Av. no. students	xx	110	xx	30	xx	105	xx	40	xx	15	xx	°

* Remedial instruction is in addition to other requirements.

Note: All periods shown are number of half-hour periods per week.

133

fundamentals, but experience indicates the probable futility of this. For many, their capacity in mathematics suggests the desirability of reducing, rather than increasing, experiences of frustration and failure. A bare minimum of time for skill maintenance is therefore planned. Those who do blossom can be shifted into the basic group; those who do not are scheduled into more profitable learning experiences.[1]

Remedial instruction time planned in Figure 9.3b is in addition to the common basic requirement. The mathematics department intends that students with ability which predicts their catching up with the basic group in grade 7, but who lack basic skills, can best be helped by assignment to extra periods of mathematics instruction. For these remedial students the additional time is in effect a temporary extra concentration in mathematics in the seventh, eighth, and ninth grades. More advanced students may at times discover remedial needs. These, however, can generally be provided for by individual study on basic skills, aided by mathematics laboratory facilities.

Decisions as to how many additional concentration periods and where to locate these in the six-year span vary according to the nature and purpose of the subject-matter area. This mathematics department plans to offer twelve additional periods for concentration to group II, locating three of these in each of the ninth, tenth, eleventh, and twelfth grades. For group III, twelve additional periods are planned, but located differently, one each in the seventh and eighth grades, two each in the ninth and tenth, and three each in the eleventh and twelfth. For group IV, concentrations total twenty-four periods, one being added in each of the seventh and eighth grades, five in each of the ninth, tenth, and twelfth grades, and seven being planned for the eleventh grade. Group IV will include the advanced placement candidates, which accounts for the strong concentration in the junior year. It must be kept in mind that within each group

---

[1] Such reassignment need not wait for semester or year-end schedule changes.

additional concentrations may vary with the individual student's needs. Some gifted students do very well and achieve high levels of breadth, depth, and mastery without additional concentrations.

The final decisions which departments make to complete Figure 9.3b reflect estimates of the number of students to plan for within each group, at each grade level. It is necessary to know how many students will fall within each group before course structure can be determined. In the bottom row of Figure 9.3b are the estimates—the average number of students in each ability and interest grouping in each grade over the six-year period. The comprehensive low-interest group (group I) initially includes 90 students, but this number is increased to 105 beginning in grade 8 with the integration of some students needing remedial instruction from grade 7. The comprehensive high-interest group stays at 30 throughout all six years (though these may not be the same students). The mathematics-talented low-interest group starts at 105 and remains the same, except for grade 9, where it drops to 90 students.

The reason for this drop is reflected in the mathematics-talented high-interest group which at grade 9 increases to 30 students from an original 15, and remains there for the balance of the six-year period. The specific variations in number are unimportant but reflect the general principle that movement of students from group to group is anticipated. The 15 students needing remedial instruction absorbed at the end of grade 9 are not added to the comprehensive low-interest group per se. Their addition will be accompanied by some movement into the mathematics-talented groups from the comprehensive groups. It is important to note that the numbers involved are only illustrative and will differ from school to school as well as from situation to situation. Each school will have a different proportion of pupils varying in ability and interest groups as well as a different total number of students.

In estimating probable enrollments in each group, the importance of teamwork between the guidance services and the curriculum departments needs to be emphasized. Curriculum decisions spell out the requirements for admitting pupils to each group; guidance services provide the evidence by which appropriate group placement can match these requirements. Guidance services must see that these groupings do not become inflexible tracks. The ideal is to achieve movement among groups as awakening interest, supported by growth in the subject, recommends. The new design encourages this shifting of group membership where responsible evidence indicates its desirability.

FIGURE 9.4. SHOWING A BASIC CURRICULUM DESIGN FOR THE ART DEPARTMENT

Grade level	GROUPS TO BE PROVIDED FOR							
	I Comprehensive low-interest basic group		II Comprehensive high interest		III Subj.-talented low interest		IV Gifted	
	No. of per.	No. of stud.	No. of per.	No. of stud.	No. of per.	No. of stud.	No. of per.	No. of stud.
Total periods base required	30	xx	30	xx	30	xx	30	xx
Additional concentration	0	xx	12	xx	24	xx	48	xx
Total periods to be scheduled	30	xx	42	xx	54	xx	78	xx
7	8	135	8	90	9	60	9	15
8	6	135	8	90	9	60	9	15
9	5	135	8	90	9	60	15	15
10	5	135	6	90	9	45	15	30
11	3	135	6	90	9	45	15	30
12	3	135	6	90	9	45	15	30
Total periods	30	xx	42	xx	54	xx	78	xx
Av. no. students	xx	135	xx	90	xx	52	xx	23

Note:
1. Four groups planned for.
2. Total enrollment each grade each year—300.
3. Increase in estimated gifted group during last three years with corresponding drop in group III.
4. Group III has two concentrations of 12 periods each—total 24.
5. Gifted group has four concentrations of 12 periods each—total 48.

FIGURE 9.5. SHOWING A BASIC CURRICULUM DESIGN FOR AN ENGLISH DEPARTMENT

Grade level	GROUPS TO BE PROVIDED FOR									
	I Comprehensive low-interest basic group		II Comprehensive high interest		III Subj.-talented low interest		IV Subj.-talented high interest		V Remedial	
	No. of per.	No. of stud.	No. of per.	No. of stud.	No. of per.	No. of stud.	No. of per.	No. of stud.	No. of per.	No. of stud.
Total periods base required	36	xx	36	xx	36	xx	36	xx	18	xx
Additional concentration	0	xx	12	xx	12	xx	24	xx	0	xx
Total periods to be scheduled	36	xx	48	xx	48	xx	60	xx	18	xx
7	8	135	8	30	12	120	12	15	3	90
8	8	120	8	30	12	120	12	30	3	75
9	6	120	8	30	6	120	9	30	3	60
10	6	120	8	30	6	120	9	30	3	45
11	4	120	8	30	6	120	9	30	3	45
12	4	105	8	30	6	120	9	45	3	30
Total periods	36	xx	48	xx	48	xx	60	xx	18°	xx
Av. no. students	xx	120	xx	30	xx	120	xx	30	xx	58°

° Remedial instruction is in addition to base requirements.

Note:
1. Five groups planned for.
2. Estimated increase in group IV with corresponding decrease in group I enrollment as students progress through high school.
3. All groups allocate more time in seventh and eighth grades except group II in allocating time, recognizing predicted growth in capacity for individual study.
4. Groups II and III have one additional concentration of 12 periods.
5. Group IV has two additional concentrations, totaling 24 periods.

Other departments build their basic design in a manner similar to the example given for mathematics. Figure 9.4 illustrates a possible design for art, Figure 9.5 for English, and Figure 9.6 for social studies.

The foregoing (as well as following) illustrations will establish models which all subject-matter areas might follow in developing basic curriculum designs which fit the overall pattern of educational

FIGURE 9.6. SHOWING A BASIC CURRICULUM DESIGN FOR A SOCIAL STUDIES DEPARTMENT

Grade level	GROUPS TO BE PROVIDED FOR									
	I Comprehensive low-interest basic group		II Comprehensive high interest		III Subj.-talented low interest		IV Subj.-talented high interest		V Gifted	
	No. of per.	No. of stud.	No. of per.	No. of stud.	No. of per.	No. of stud.	No. of per.	No. of stud.	No. of per.	No. of stud.
Total periods base required	30	xx	30	xx	30	xx	30	xx	30	xx
Additional concentration	0	xx	12	xx	24	xx	36	xx	60	xx
Total periods to be scheduled	30	xx	42	xx	54	xx	66	xx	90	xx
7	5	120	7	15	7	120	7	30	15	15
8	5	120	7	15	7	120	7	30	15	15
9	5	105	8	30	8	120	8	30	15	15
10	5	105	8	30	10	120	13	30	15	15
11	5	105	8	30	11	120	15	30	15	15
12	5	105	8	30	11	120	16	30	15	15
Total periods	30	xx	42	xx	54	xx	66	xx	90	xx
Av. no. students	xx	110	xx	25	xx	120	xx	30	xx	15

Note:
1. Group II has one additional concentration of 12 periods.
2. Group III has two additional concentrations, totaling 24 periods.
3. Group IV has three additional concentrations, totaling 36 periods.
4. Group V has five additional concentrations, totaling 60 periods.
5. The department estimates 5 per cent of students at each grade level will elect the gifted program (0.05 × 300 = 15).
6. The number who are subject-talented but low interest are predicted to be constant over the six years.
7. Group I maintains a 2½-hour-per-week schedule throughout the six years, a different policy from that shown in the mathematics, art, and English departmental designs.

area allocation shown in Figure 9.2d. Again let it be emphasized that the groupings shown are suggestions, not necessities. The actual groupings evolve from local situations. Many other possible arrangements exist, arrangements perhaps better suited to a particular school.

Figure 9.7 shows a conceptual illustration of how the time allocation over the high school span shifts from required time for all toward more and more variations to satisfy individual student growth. Individual departments contribute to this overall pattern in different ways. All should keep the general pattern in mind as they plan.

The foregoing decisions and those which follow require cooperative planning by curriculum staff, including the teachers, and the skill with which this planning is done will vitally affect the success of any innovations acted upon. The new design offers a model to guide this planning (see Figure 9.8). This model suggests the

FIGURE 9.7. VARIATION IN CURRICULUM EMPHASIS ACCORDING TO
PUPIL INTERESTS AND ABILITIES

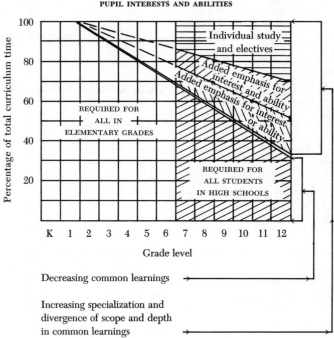

Decreasing common learnings →

Increasing specialization and
divergence of scope and depth
in common learnings →

A question for departmental inquiry:
Are grade-level lines necessary in the
secondary school? If so, why?

FIGURE 9.8. PHASES IN THE COOPERATIVE DEVELOPMENT OF
NEW DESIGN CURRICULUMS

Phase I
1. Select basic study groups.
2. Share ideas and common concerns.
3. Discuss basic curricular framework.

Phase II
4. Consult with area experts regarding framework.
5. Delineate student groups.
6. Agree upon competences to be stressed.
7. Report suggested competences to other subject groups for possible correlation.

Phase III
8. Consult with subject specialists regarding appropriate content vehicles for competences sought.
9. Write a broad scope and sequence.

Phase IV
10. Define with subject expert the specific content determined to be necessary for competence desired.
11. Prepare course units for each group and grade level.
12. Relate to a body of theory for teaching and learning.

Phase V
13. Guide experimental classroom application of curriculum.
14. Evaluate results and modify as appropriate.

An ongoing process

sequential steps by which professional teams may implement new designs in local contexts. Administrative responsibilities include provision of time both for this planning and for favorably acknowledging it.

Departmental Development of Course Structure

The basic curriculum framework having been determined, the next step involves departmental staff in decisions answering such questions as these:

1. What specific courses will achieve the aims for each of the groups at each grade level? How do specific course aims integrate with general sequential objectives of the department?

2. What course structure, adapted to the weekly time module, will best accomplish specific course aims? What phases of instruction are planned? Small group? Large group? Laboratory? Individual work?

These decisions require appraisal of such variables as available staff; methods predicted to be most efficient and effective; class-size possibilities related to method, facilities, and material resources available; financial limitations; staff-utilization possibilities; and supporting, nonprofessional assistance.

Chapter 3 illustrated a variety of course structures which might be planned within the limitations of a weekly time module. Examples applying this concept to a specific course will now be given. The basic curriculum designs illustrated in Figures 9.3a and 9.3b set the limits within which these course structures can be developed.

Sample Structures for Mathematics Instruction   Referring to Figure 9.3b, this mathematics department has allocated five periods of instructional time weekly for the ninth-grade comprehensive low-interest group (basic group I). The department must accommodate 105 ninth graders in this group plus any others from other grades who may be accelerated for concentration purposes. In this instance the mathematics department estimates that there will be 15 gifted students from the seventh-grade group who can profitably participate in ninth-grade instruction, and so they plan for 105 + 15 or 120 students.

Two types of instruction are seen to meet well the instructional aims for these 120 students: a large-group type and a laboratory type. The large group will bring all 120 students, a total of eight class-size models, together in one section three times a week for half-hour periods. This section takes three of the five instructional periods allocated in the departmental design for ninth-grade mathematics, group I. The remaining periods of one-half hour each will be devoted to laboratory instruction. Twenty-four students can be taken care of in each laboratory section. So five sections, meeting one-half hour twice a week, are required to accommodate 105 ninth graders plus 15 accelerated seventh graders.

The weekly course cycle for ninth-grade mathematics thus requires each student to participate in three one-half-hour large-group instructional phases and two one-half-hour laboratory phases. It should be remembered that this does not include time for individual study. Figure 9.9a gives a graphic representation of the ninth-grade mathematics structure for group I.

Figure 9.9b shows the mathematics-course structure planned for group IV, the twelfth-grade subject-talented, high-interest group. This group has been allocated 8 periods of instruction per week in the departmental design. These are distributed in five weekly meetings as a group of 45 and three weekly laboratory sessions of the same size. The large sections portray confidence in this group's individual members' capacity to direct their own efforts with a minimum of individual supervision. Several other interesting course structures could be planned for group IV, examples of which are: The 45 students might be scheduled in phase A, which brings them all

FIGURE **9.9a.** STRUCTURE AND STAFF FOR
NINTH-GRADE MATHEMATICS, GROUP I

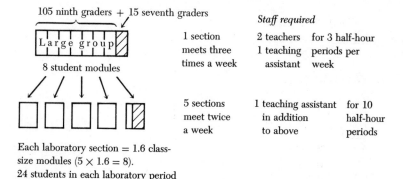

105 ninth graders + 15 seventh graders

8 student modules

Staff required

1 section meets three times a week	2 teachers 1 teaching assistant	for 3 half-hour periods per week
5 sections meet twice a week	1 teaching assistant in addition to above	for 10 half-hour periods

Each laboratory section = 1.6 class-size modules (5 × 1.6 = 8).
24 students in each laboratory period

Comparing above with traditional structure (for 120 students):

	Facilities required	*Staff required*	*Time per week per student*
As proposed above—	1 large-group room—capacity 120 students; 1 laboratory—capacity 45 students	2 teachers 2 teaching assts. 7½ hours of instruction per week	2½ hours or 5 periods per week
Traditional structure—	4 classrooms— capacity 30 each	4 teachers 20 hours of instruction per week	5 hours or 10 periods per week

together for one hour, two periods, once a week; in phase B, which brings them together for one-half hour in small-group sections of 15, three times a week; in phase C, which plans 3 half-hour periods of individual study or laboratory weekly to complete the 8-period allocation.

The structure designed by this mathematics department for ninth-grade remedial students is interesting as it shows how some course phases can serve several grades or several groups at one grade level.

FIGURE 9.9*b*. STRUCTURE AND STAFF FOR
TWELFTH-GRADE MATHEMATICS, GROUP IV

1 section of
45 students
meets 5 times
a week

Staff required
1 teacher—for 5 half-hour periods

3 student modules

1 laboratory of
45 students
meets 3 times
a week

1 teacher   } for 3
1 teaching asst. } half-hour periods

3 student modules

Comparing above with traditional structure (for 45 high-ability, high-interest seniors):

	Facilities required	*Staff required*	*Time per week per student*
As proposed above—	1 mathematics classroom— capacity 45; 1 mathematics laboratory— capacity 45	2 teachers 1 teaching asst. 4 hours of instruction per week	4 hours or 8 periods per week
Traditional structure—	2 mathematics classrooms— capacity 30 each 1 laboratory section	2 teachers 10 hours of instruction per week	5 hours or 10 half-hour periods per week

Remember that the basic departmental design requires all remedial students to participate in the group I program already illustrated in Figure 9.9*a*, which takes up 5 periods weekly. The 15 ninth-grade remedial students are thus already scheduled for three large-group phases each week and two small-group sessions, totaling 2½ hours of instruction. The additional three periods of remedial work are taken care of by assignment to a remedial laboratory section, meeting one-half hour, three times a week. Since this laboratory can easily accommodate more than 15 students, 15 additional students from other *groups* or *grades* can be assigned to this same section. Figure 9.9*c* illustrates this remedial structure for group VI, ninth grade.

The nature of the structure planned for remedial groups will vary somewhat with the number of students identified as needing remedial concentration. If in all six grades a maximum of 30 to 45 students was anticipated, two phases might adequately handle them all together, as illustrated in Figure 9.9*d*. Here an intern, a teaching assistant, and a senior teacher who is a specialist in remedial instruction can take care of all grades. The senior teacher meets once a week with a large section of 45 remedial students from all grades. The intern and teaching assistant meet twice a week for half-hour laboratory periods with the same group.

FIGURE 9.9*c*. SHOWING STRUCTURE FOR
NINTH-GRADE REMEDIAL GROUP IN MATHEMATICS

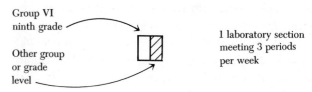

Group VI
ninth grade

Other group
or grade
level

1 laboratory section
meeting 3 periods
per week

30 students, 15 of whom are ninth graders, group VI, and 15 of whom may be from other grades, or laboratory period of other groups

Group I
large-group
course phase

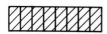

Large-group
sections
meet 3 times a week

This is regular phase for all ninth graders in group I.

Group I
laboratory
phase

5 regular laboratory sections
of 24 students each
group I

Meets ½ hour
2 times a week

The 15 ninth-grade remedial students attend the regularly scheduled phases with group I. In addition they have 3 extra laboratory periods each week.

FIGURE 9.9*d*. SHOWING ANOTHER STRUCTURE FOR FORTY-FIVE OR FEWER
REMEDIAL STUDENTS—GRADES 7 TO 12

Remedial class		1 section meeting ½ hour per week	Taught by a senior teacher
Remedial laboratory		1 section meeting 2 periods per week	

Each phase includes three student modules, totaling 45 students. The above 45 students would be scheduled also in the course structure for group I of their grade levels.

The possibility of combining groups from different grades in some course phases in mathematics merits further exploration. For example, group I of the eleventh grade will enroll an estimated 105 students (see Figure 9.9*b*). Group IV of the eighth grade, subject-talented, high interest, will enroll an estimated 45 students. The eleventh graders could be scheduled with the eighth graders (as shown in Figure 9.9*e*) for the large-group phase of the course requiring three half-hour periods a week. Such scheduling would take care of the basic eleventh-grade requirement. The eighth graders have five additional half-hour periods which will be devoted to a laboratory of one hour, meeting once a week, a small-group session of one hour meeting once a week, and a short laboratory of one-half hour meeting once a week.

In Chapter 8 the importance of facility modifications to implementation of the new design was discussed and examples were given showing how special facilities may be scheduled in various ways to encourage their full use. The above course structures for mathematics groups require a special mathematics laboratory. Although it is not the basic purpose of this book to present descriptions of facility innovations, one mathematics laboratory, designed by Arthur Weibe, president of Pacific College, Fresno, California, will be described.

FIGURE 9.9e. SHOWING INTEGRATION OF A GROUP I
ELEVENTH-GRADE COURSE PHASE WITH A GROUP IV
EIGHTH-GRADE PHASE IN MATHEMATICS

105 eleventh graders
group I

Phase A
large group
150 students
15 stud. modules

1 section   Staff
3 times   1 senior
a week   teacher

45 eighth graders
group IV

The above completes the group I requirement for eleventh graders. The eighth graders continue in the course phase each week.

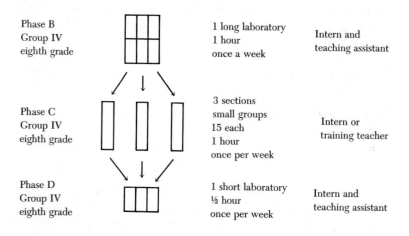

Phase B
Group IV
eighth grade

1 long laboratory
1 hour
once a week

Intern and
teaching assistant

Phase C
Group IV
eighth grade

3 sections
small groups
15 each
1 hour
once per week

Intern or
training teacher

Phase D
Group IV
eighth grade

1 short laboratory
½ hour
once per week

Intern and
teaching assistant

Phase A—Combines seven student modules of eleventh graders in group I with three student modules of eighth graders in group IV into one large group, meeting one-half hour three times a week.

Phase B—Once a week the forty-five eighth graders in group IV meet in a one-hour (two-period) laboratory session.

Phase C—Once a week the eighth graders in group IV meet in small groups of fifteen students for one hour.

Phase D—Completes the eighth-grade group IV structure with one short laboratory of one half-hour meeting once a week, with forty-five students.

A Proposed Mathematics Laboratory Facility (See Figure 9.10)

Programmed Learning Area   The programmed learning area provides for sixteen individual stations, completely equipped for machine learning or for individual study. These offer a ready "extra" for each module in the event of operational difficulties. Replacement equipment is immediately available in the storage area (B).

The staffing for the laboratory provides for three persons for each period: a teacher or intern, a teaching assistant, and a clerk. The teacher or intern is in charge of two modules but concentrates on helping students in the small-group study area and in the laboratory. The teaching assistant works under the direction of the teacher, but primarily in the same areas. A clerk handles the operation of the program control center under the direction of the teacher. This center is so designed that the sequence of programs for each student is electronically determined.

Program Control Center (A)   This center is completely automated. These are the major features:

1. There is visual contact with each booth.

2. There is individual electronic communication with each learner.

3. A control panel shows individual programs in progress, rate of student progress, rate of error, etc., for each of the stations. This information is coded and stored on the memory drums of the computer for future reference.

4. The computer-programmer has in storage all available records for each student including standardized achievement tests, performances on various programs, intelligence tests, programs completed, rate of progress, level or quality of performance, etc. The com-

FIGURE 9.10. A PROPOSED MATHEMATICS LABORATORY

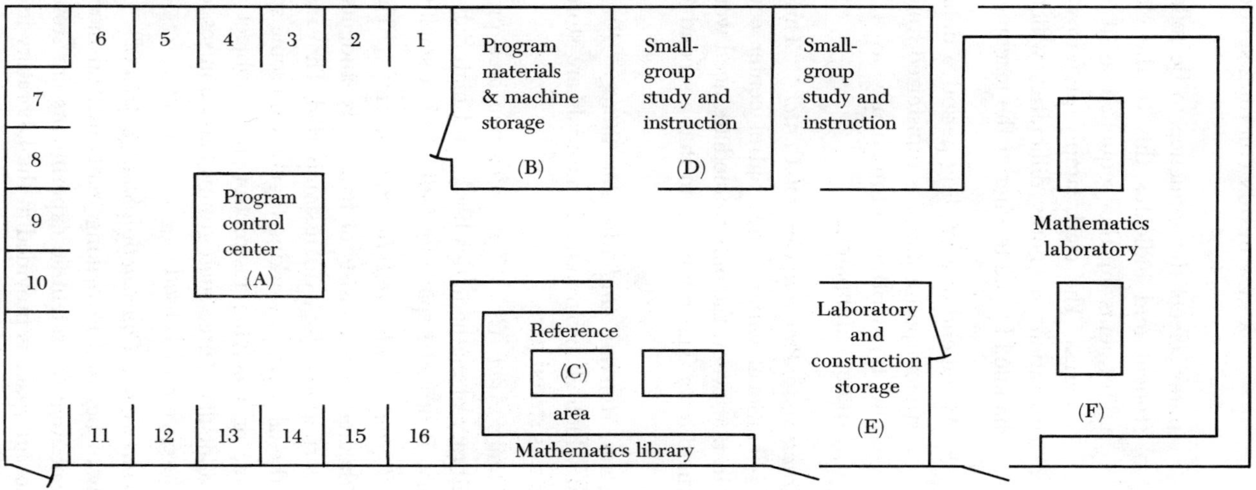

puter selects the sequence to be followed by each student and indicates this to the clerk. It makes adjustments in the sequence as it notes student progress. The clerk simply performs the indicated operations or notes difficulties which need to be handled by the teacher or the teaching assistant.

5. At the end of a grading period, a detailed record of student performance is transferred from the machine and typewritten automatically as a report to the student and parents.

Alternative to Program Control Center   This center could become operational without the control center equipped as described. In that event, the only immediate need would be to have programmed texts. This might mean that a second clerk would be added.

Program Materials and Machine Storage (B)   This is the center in which all programmed materials are stored. Additional equipment is stored here.

Reference Area (C)   The reference area provides a small branch library of mathematics books and materials needed in the laboratory. It provides space for individual or small-group study.

Small-group Study and Instruction (D)   The small-group study indicated here consists of five or six students gathering for special instruction or for a discussion period. They may be planning work in the laboratory, working together on some special program or project, or receiving instruction in a subject area which is causing difficulty. Three such groups can be in session at one time if the reference area is used.

Laboratory and Construction Storage Area (E)   Construction materials to be used in making mathematical models and larger equipment used for scientific experiments are stored here. Additional storage space is provided in the laboratory itself.

Mathematics Laboratory (F)   This is the work area for the construction of models, applications of mathematics to physical objects, performance of scientific experiments which illustrate the application of mathematics, and use of various computational machines by individual pupils. In this total program there would be close cooperation between the science department and the mathematics department. Science and mathematics teachers would work in close liaison with each other.

Laboratories for Other Subject-matter Areas   Departments will find the mathematics laboratory discussed above illustrates specialized adaptation of form to serve function in education. A variety of interesting designs are available, serving science, art, English, business education, social studies, and languages. Those interested may wish to write to the School Planning Laboratory, Stanford University, for new laboratory facility designs and information on schools where they may be observed in operation. The use of modern electronic aids and self-study teaching devices should be considered when planning facilities for all subject-matter areas.

The design of course structures in other subject-matter fields parallels that illustrated for mathematics. Specific examples for an arts course, an English course, and a social studies course will be briefly described.

The Structure of an Arts Course   Referring to Figure 9.4 gives the time allocation of nine periods for group III subject-talented, high-interest students. At the ninth-grade level sixty students are planned for in this group. These will be interested in several different media: instrumental or choral music, painting, drawing, crafts, home economics, industrial arts, or business office crafts. To develop these various talents and interests, several types of specialized laboratories are provided in the practical, visual, and performing-arts center. There are facilities for

1. Drawing, painting, and applied design

2. Home arts and small crafts, such as interior decoration, costume design, weaving, ceramics, small art metals

3. Three-dimensional design and production, cabinetmaking, and metalworking

4. Theater arts, stage design, drama

5. Instrumental music

6. Choral music

7. A foods and consumer laboratory

8. Dressmaking and sewing

9. An arts library and visual-resource center

10. A business office crafts laboratory, including typewriters, office machines, duplicators, transcribers, electronic office equipment for data processing and recording

Course phases planned will necessarily include more than one of the four arts and crafts groups and will cut across all grade levels. Sequences planned will be according to talent and interest in the media rather than by grade level. This approach will predictably make the arts and crafts program much more stimulating and attractive, both for the basic group I and for those desiring concentration. Students may change from one medium to another as interest develops, or may plan diversified experiences in one, two, or three media.

Figure 9.11 illustrates one possible structure to take care of sixty ninth graders in group III arts and crafts who have special talents in eight different media. It is well to remember the basic curriculum design for the whole school in analyzing this structure. Every student, whatever his group or grade, is required to devote five instructional periods a week to one of the visual, performing, or practical arts. Beyond this some will add concentration periods. In

FIGURE 9.11. SHOWING A POSSIBLE STRUCTURE TO TAKE CARE OF
SIXTY NINTH-GRADE STUDENTS, GROUP III, ARTS AND CRAFTS MEDIA

Assuming these enrollments according to eight different media:

1. Wood or metal crafts 10
2. Foods or clothing crafts 10
3. Business office crafts 5
4. Drama-theater art 5
5. Instrumental music 10
6. Vocal music 10
7. Painting and drawing 5
8. Art metal, ceramics,
   sculpture 5

   Total 60

Phase A
time modules
two periods
weekly

A large group in each of eight media, meeting ½ hour, twice a week. Students from other groups and grades make up the majority of this group membership.

Students from other groups and grades interested in this media

Students from group III, ninth grade

Phase B
time modules
six periods
weekly

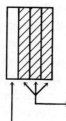

A 1½-hour laboratory period twice a week, in eight different media. This will include individual laboratory and small-group work based on the nature of the media. The sixty ninth graders will be distributed among the eight media according to the enrollment shown above.

Students from other groups and grades

Students from group III, ninth grade

Phase C
time module
one period
weekly

A ½-hour period for individual study or concentration. May be in library art center or in laboratory according to media and student. Is not scheduled with any organized group.

The sixty students report to the arts center for each phase of their course where they will be assigned to the appropriate phases according to the media of their special talent and interest.

the example illustrated there are three of these periods for sixty ninth graders. The distribution according to media is hypothetical here. It might vary from school to school and certainly will be affected by laboratory facilities provided. Gifted students, in group IV, might be best taken care of by having them follow, with group III, phases A and B, and extend phase C to cover more time modules per week.

A Course Structure in Ninth-grade English   The English department basic design shown in Figure 9.5 allocates six periods weekly and estimates 120 students for group V. The Language Arts Committee on Flexible Scheduling and Curriculum Organization in Los Angeles County[1] has developed a design which illustrates how English departments can depart from the example of Figure 9.5. This design plans for four groups rather than five: comprehensive, talented, gifted, and limited. The course structure developed by this committee for a unit in paragraph development, group I, grade 9, is shown in Figure 9.12. A total of 120 students is planned for. Eight weekly time modules are allocated rather than the six shown for the similar group in Figure 9.5. Three course phases are planned: (1) a large-group lecture of 8-student modules—120 students, ½ hour, meeting twice a week; (2) small-group sections of 15 students (1 student module), ½ hour, meeting three times a week; and (3) individual study sections in groups of 30 (2 student modules), meeting for ½ hour, three times a week.

A staff of four teachers and two teacher aids forms a team for this instructional responsibility. The team devotes four hours of instructional time to this assignment. A traditional structure of 5 one-hour sections of 30 students each per week would require a staff of 4 teachers and take five hours of their time, or two teachers for ten hours, or one teacher for twenty hours.

---

[1] Howard Waymire, *A Proposal for Flexible Scheduling and Curriculum Organization*, Language Arts, Los Angeles County Schools, 1961.

FIGURE 9.12. SHOWING NINTH-GRADE COMPREHENSIVE GROUP
COURSE STRUCTURE IN ENGLISH FOR 120 STUDENTS
(DESIGNED BY LOS ANGELES COUNTY SCHOOLS)

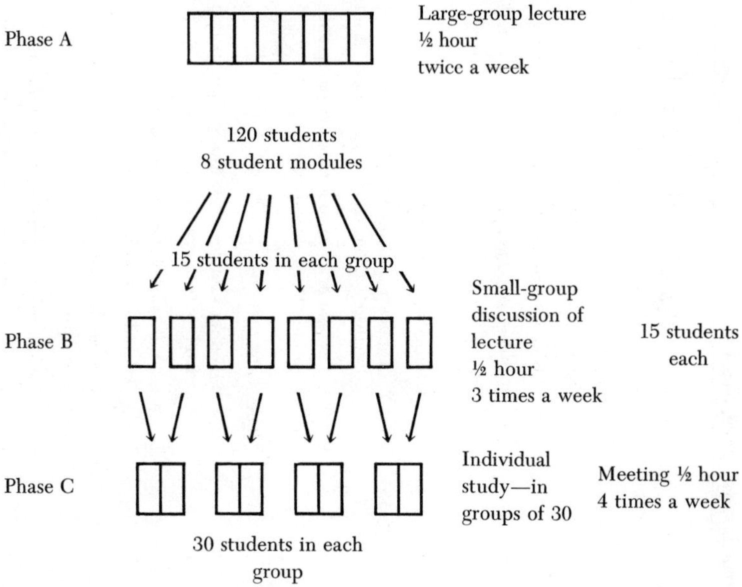

Phase A

Large-group lecture
½ hour
twice a week

120 students
8 student modules

15 students in each group

Phase B

Small-group
discussion of
lecture
½ hour
3 times a week

15 students
each

Phase C

Individual
study—in
groups of 30

Meeting ½ hour
4 times a week

30 students in each
group

The staff required for the three phases:
A team of four teachers, two assistants for four hours of instruction per week

Traditional practice would require:
A staff of four teachers to devote five hours of instruction per week or one teacher for
twenty hours each week

The Los Angeles County English Committee which designed this
structure relates the objectives to each phase of a week's instruction
in paragraph development as shown in Figure 9.13. This illustrates
very well the importance of designing course structure from a consideration of types of instruction most suitable to staff, facilities,
objectives, and methodology.

FIGURE 9.13. WRITTEN EXPRESSION—PARAGRAPH DEVELOPMENT

COMPREHENSIVE GROUP, GRADE 9

Objectives	Obj. no.	Sample instructional procedures	Time mod.
1. Recognize main ideas and supporting details.		*Large group*	
2. Recognize different types of paragraph development.	1	Demonstration—lectures	
		1. Elements of a paragraph: main idea and details.	2
3. Develop skill in writing well-developed paragraphs.	2	2. Types of paragraphs: examples and details.	
4. Develop skill in writing various types of paragraphs.	1	*Small group*	
		1. Discussion of paragraph analysis.	
	1	2. Application of paragraph analysis (analyze various teacher-furnished paragraphs).	3
	2	3. Discussion of various types of paragraphs. Recognition of types from samples.	
		Independent study	
	1	1. Gather samples of well-developed paragraphs from outside sources.	
	2	2. Find examples of paragraphs developed by details and example.	3
	3, 4	3. Write paragraphs developed by details and example.	
		4. Continue independent study projects.	

A Sample Structure for a Ninth-grade Social Studies Course
In Figure 9.6 a basic curriculum design for social studies allocated
five periods of instruction weekly to group I and estimates an
enrollment of 105 students in the ninth grade. A total of 300 ninth
graders in all five groups is planned for. The department has
designed a course structure for group I made up of four phases in
a weekly cycle (Figure 9.14).

All 300 students from all groups are brought together once a week
for ½ hour. This requires an auditorium large enough to house the
total group. The next phase involves group I and group II together
in a ½-hour meeting of 135 students once a week. In the third phase
group I students meet in small groups of 15 each, requiring 7 sections, one hour long, once a week. The final phase places these
students in a laboratory of one hour which meets once a week.
Here there are two sections of 60 students each, including a small
number from group II of the seventh grade.

Staffing of this structure will require one period of ½ hour from
a teacher and two teacher aids for phase A, a teacher and one teacher
aid for ½ hour for phase B, 3½ hours of teacher time to lead the
seven small groups in phase C, and ½ hour of a teacher and
a teacher aid for phase D, the laboratory period. Such will be
the weekly time commitment of staff. Contrast this with the traditional course structure: for 105 ninth graders three teachers one
hour daily five days a week, totaling fifteen hours of teacher time
weekly.

Facilities required are a well-equipped auditorium of 300 capacity, a large-group classroom of 120 capacity, seven small-group
discussion areas, and a special social studies laboratory housing 60
students. This latter is seen as perhaps the only unit not readily
usable by other departments in the school.

Other structures are possible. For example, the social studies
department in the Whittier Union High School, Whittier, California,
has planned a two-phase structure for their ninth grade, group I.
They have estimated an enrollment of 85 students in this group,

FIGURE 9.14. SHOWING A POSSIBLE COURSE STRUCTURE FOR GROUP I,
NINTH-GRADE SOCIAL STUDIES

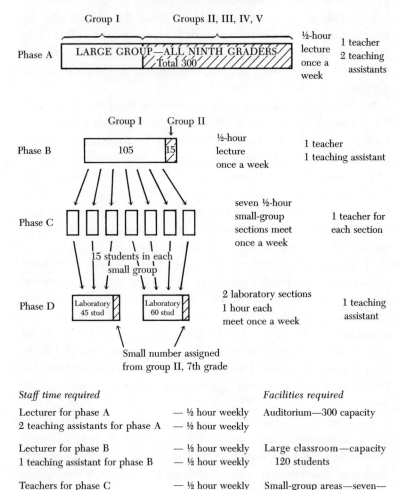

Staff time required		Facilities required
Lecturer for phase A	— ½ hour weekly	Auditorium—300 capacity
2 teaching assistants for phase A	— ½ hour weekly	
Lecturer for phase B	— ½ hour weekly	Large classroom—capacity
1 teaching assistant for phase B	— ½ hour weekly	120 students
Teachers for phase C	— ½ hour weekly	Small-group areas—seven—
7 sections	each section,	15 capacity each
	3½ total	
Teacher assistant for phase D	— 1 hour weekly	Large social studies laboratory— capacity 60 students

FIGURE 9.15. A COURSE PHASE PLANNED FOR GROUP I, NINTH-GRADE
SOCIAL STUDIES, WHITTIER UNION HIGH SCHOOL, WHITTIER, CALIFORNIA
85 STUDENTS

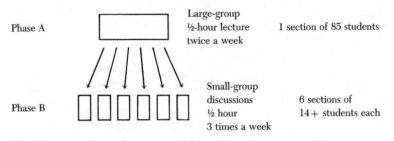

Phase A — Large-group ½-hour lecture twice a week — 1 section of 85 students

Phase B — Small-group discussions ½ hour 3 times a week — 6 sections of 14 + students each

Total periods of scheduled instruction per week—5

and plan on a base requirement of 5 periods a week.[1]

In phase A, all 85 students meet for ½ hour in a large group, two times a week. In phase B, the students meet three times a week in small groups of 15 each, for ½ hour. See Figure 9.15. During the 36-week year the tentative allocation of time to five general topics is as follows:

Topics	Total weeks of study
School-community	2
Vocation	7
Personality	7
World geography	12
Introduction to history	8
	36

Figure 9.16 shows how the Whittier department structure for group III varies from the basic group. Here a concentration of seven additional periods weekly has been planned. Two additional ½-hour lectures (large-group), one additional small-group discussion of ½ hour, and four scheduled ½-hour periods of individual study

[1] Helen H. Holloway, *A Progress Report of the Flexible Scheduling Study Committee for Social Studies*, Whittier Union High School District, Whittier, Calif., 1962.

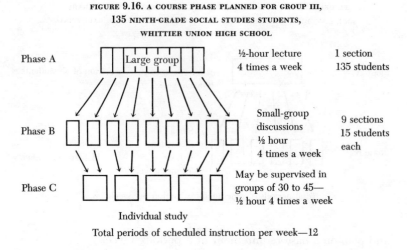

FIGURE 9.16. A COURSE PHASE PLANNED FOR GROUP III,
135 NINTH-GRADE SOCIAL STUDIES STUDENTS,
WHITTIER UNION HIGH SCHOOL

Phase A — Large group — ½-hour lecture / 4 times a week — 1 section / 135 students

Phase B — Small-group discussions / ½ hour / 4 times a week — 9 sections / 15 students each

Phase C — May be supervised in groups of 30 to 45— / ½ hour 4 times a week

Individual study

Total periods of scheduled instruction per week—12

complete the seven periods of instruction added to the basic program for group I.

Tentative plans at Whittier assign a team of 4 teachers to each grade level, each team led by a master teacher. These teams plan the most appropriate assignments for large-group, small-group, and individual study responsibilities. Weekly classroom loads for each teacher vary from fourteen to sixteen hours of instructional time. Usually all members of each team participate with at least one student group in all course phases—large-group, small-group, and individual instruction.

The foregoing illustrations of departmental decisions defining the structure of specific courses will serve to clarify the general nature of this process for all areas of study. As has been seen, interwoven with course structuring are decisions as to staff assignment. Now, for answers to the question, "What teachers and supporting staff are necessary?" suggestions will be offered, with illustrations, supplementing the discussion in Chapter 5.

10

EXAMPLES OF THE NEW DESIGN: COMPUTING STAFF REQUIREMENTS

The Importance of a Professional Decision prior to Computation

Before staff requirements can be calculated for any instructional group or total department, this basic question must be answered:

For any course, assuming four phases, and considering numbers enrolled, what staff is required to accomplish the aims effectively and efficiently during each phase?

Effectiveness relates to degree of achievement of the aims for which the course was organized; efficiency relates to the costs of materials, of human energy, and of time in reaching these aims. It is quite possible to decrease efficiency while seeking to improve effectiveness, and vice versa. For some course phases large-group instruction is highly effective and efficient, while in other course phases such instruction may be highly efficient, but relatively ineffective in terms of goals achieved. Likewise some small-group instruction may be quite effective but highly inefficient for specific goals and individual instruction for many purposes can be predictably effective, yet its costs in terms of both instructional time and use of special equipment may become too high.

The answer to the basic question raised above has been given in part when a course structure has been decided, as illustrated in many examples heretofore. Another part of the answer is given when the number of senior teachers, teachers, interns, teaching assistants, and clerks considered necessary to conduct a course, or a complete departmental design for a particular group, has been determined. Once such a departmental staff or team has been organized, it is presumed that considerations of effectiveness and of efficiency by professional, experienced teachers and administrators have guided the decisions.

These are professional decisions. They cannot be made by those not experienced and not expert in the particular domain of knowledge to which they apply. If one asks, "How much and what kind of professional and support staff is necessary to accomplish well (effectively and efficiently) the aims of a large-group phase consisting of 300 students in tenth-grade social studies?" one must seek the answer and the evidence to support it from experienced experts in social studies teaching. The answer is, of course, subject to testing of practice. The answer given for social studies groups may well be different from that for physical education, English, mathematics, or science instruction. It depends on exactly what kinds of things are done, what tools are provided to those who act, and what time is necessary to use these tools well and to measure accurately the results.

Traditional practice has made such decisions since schools began. More or less uniform for all areas of knowledge has been the assumption that to teach any high school subject effectively and efficiently one teacher is required for every 30 students and that this teacher should meet five classes of 30 students each five days per week. Administrators point with pride to their pupil-teacher ratio and believe that success is theirs if they can keep this ratio within the range of one teacher for every 28 to 32 students in their building. Recognition has been given to supporting, nonteaching staff such as counselors, deans, and supervisors; and gradually these have tended to pull the ratio down, sometimes even to 24 or 25 pupils for every certified teacher. Too often when this is done, the actual effect has been to raise class size per teacher, for administration rarely escapes from the financial straitjacket of an annual budget.

The new design requires a fresh look at this pupil-teacher ratio tradition. The optimal ratio for large-group instruction, for laboratory instruction, and other course phases does not adapt to traditional interpretations. Necessarily, the introduction of teaching assistants and clerical support staff further undermines the validity of a general 1-teacher-to-every-30-pupils assumption. Administration still must convert the total staff required into some unit by which budgetary planning can be done. This will require the recognition of different load factors for different kinds of staff and instructional assignments, as the conversion occurs. The new design proposes a "teacher equivalent" concept for this purpose, which will replace the traditional "pupil-teacher ratio" standard for budget planning.

The Concept of One Full-time Load   Whether one is a clerk, a teaching assistant, an intern, or a member of the professional staff, one needs a defined basic-load standard. The specifications given in Figure 9.1 provide one good definition of this. For both supporting and professional staff, a full load is here defined as 80 time modules per week. This becomes the weekly time commitment of all staff for full-load status. It includes 5 time modules for lunch. Traditionally a full load has been defined in terms of seven hours daily for teachers and eight hours daily for noncertified personnel. These time units have been in hours per day. The new design proposes a full-load concept in terms of number of half-hour periods per week, which would ordinarily distribute into 16 periods per day, but not necessarily so.

The Concept of Staff-load Module   One staff-load module equals one-half hour of responsibility. Thus a teacher who is assigned to a course phase meeting one hour (2 periods) twice a week assumes $2 \times 2 = 4$ staff-load modules of responsibility. An intern, assigned to a laboratory phase meeting 1½ hours, three times a week, assumes $3 \times 3 = 9$ staff-load modules of responsibility. A teaching assistant assigned to a large-group phase of a course, meeting ½ hour, three times a week, assumes $1 \times 3 = 3$ staff-load modules of responsibility. A clerk, assigned to a departmental team for three hours daily, assumes $5 \times 6 = 30$ staff modules of responsibility. The staff module is thus equal to $\frac{1}{80}$ of the full-time load. Staff-load modules are merely the basic time blocks for building the total weekly time load.

The Concept of One Full Instructional Load　　How many staff-load modules make up one full instructional load? The answer here should vary according to the category of staff (teacher, intern, or teacher assistant) doing the instruction. A basic assumption about teachers gives them more responsibility per period of instruction than the intern or teacher assistant. Recognizing this, the new design suggests the following instructional load definition:

> 50 staff-load modules = 1 full instructional load for
> teachers per week
> 54 staff-load modules = 1 full instructional load for
> interns per week
> 60 staff-load modules = 1 full instructional load for
> teacher assistants per week

The rationale for the above is mainly the assumption that the professional teacher has greater responsibilities in staff meetings, planning, guidance, contacts with parents, etc., than the other two categories of staff do. The above definitions are only suggestions and provide a start upon which to base further inquiry.

The Concept of One Full Support Load, Professional Personnel This concept derives from the foregoing concept of one full instructional load when related to the full-time responsibility of 80 periods a week. Time devoted by professional staff to departmental and general faculty meetings, to guidance groups, to planning and evaluation is considered as support load. Subtracting 5 periods for lunch each week from the 80-period total leaves 75 periods of responsibility to be divided between instruction and support load. Subtracting the full instructional load for each category of professional staff gives the following full support load assumptions:

Full support load for a teacher: $75 - 50 = 25$ periods per week
Full support load for an intern: $75 - 54 = 21$ periods per week
Full support load for a teacher aid: $75 - 60 = 15$ periods per week

These become the periods to be devoted to *support* rather than to instructional responsibilities each week, *if the staff member is carrying a full instructional load.* To the extent that the instructional load is reduced below the full-load standards given for either the teacher, the intern, or the teacher assistant, his support load responsibilities can be increased accordingly, assuming that he is working full time as a member of the faculty.

The Concept of One Full Support Load for Clerical Staff Since clerical staff accept no instructional responsibilities, one full support load for a clerk $= 80 - 5$ periods for lunch or 75 periods of clerical responsibility per week.

The Concept of Total Staff Modules for a Particular Department Each department plans large-group, laboratory, and small-group phases of instructional load responsibility. Each department distributes this responsibility among *instructional* and *supporting* staff as it makes its staff-utilization decisions. An example of this is shown in Figure 10.1, under the column headed "Total staff modules." The numbers here represent the total of half-hour periods for which each *category* of staff has responsibility during the weekly cycle. English teachers are committed to 10 periods of large-group instruction during the week, English interns to 1, and teaching assistants to 11. Teacher assistants contribute 20 periods weekly to support of large-group instruction, 140 periods to support of laboratory instruction, no periods to support of small-group instruction. Clerks are assigned no instructional load responsibilities, etc. It should be noted that teacher assistants carry *both* instructional and support responsibilities.

The Concept of Instructional Weight Ratio for a Particular Department Time alone does not adequately measure load. What activities and responsibilities occur during a given period of instructional time? How do these affect the load of the teacher, intern, or teacher assistant? How can such variables be recognized? How can the load of a teacher lecturing for one-half hour to a group of 300 English students in the auditorium be compared with the load of a teacher leading a half-hour small-group discussion involving 15 English students or with the load of a teacher directing an English laboratory of 45 students for one-half hour? Answers to these questions are not easy, and perhaps the answers vary from department to department. But a start must be made. The new design introduces the following weight ratios to recognize such load differentials:

	Weight ratio
Large-group instruction	2.0
Small-group instruction	1.5
Laboratory instruction	1.0

In effect the above ratios set the half-hour period of laboratory instruction as the basic load unit and adjust the other types of instructional load to this as follows:

$$\frac{\text{Load for large-group instruction per period}}{\text{Load for laboratory instruction per period}} = 2.0$$

$$\frac{\text{Load for small-group instruction per period}}{\text{Load for laboratory instruction per period}} = 1.5$$

Such recognition of load variance may be quite untenable when applied to local school situations, and if so, the ratios can be adjusted. This is a decision for *competent professional teachers* and administrators to make together. The nature of the supporting staff used and the kinds of technological tools provided will be a vital influence in the search for fair load-ratio differentials.

The column headed "Instruction weight ratio" in Figure 10.1 illustrates the above ratios as applied to each category of staff and to each kind of instruction in the English department.

The Concept of Total Staff Factors   This is the product of the total staff modules assigned to a particular category of staff and instructional method by the instruction weight ratio just described. It converts the total staff modules to staff factors more nearly equal in terms of actual load.

If

M = total staff modules
R = instructional weight ratio
F = staff factors

then $MR = F$

These conversions are shown in the column headed "Total staff factors" in Figure 10.1.

Assumptions of Teacher Equivalent Ratios Related to Salary Salary differentials of course affect budgets and therefore affect staff-utilization decisions. The new design assumes that generally an intern can be employed for two-thirds of the basic teacher's salary, a teaching assistant for one-half of the professional's salary, and a clerk for two-fifths of this salary. These relationships are expressed as teacher equivalents (previously referred to in Chapter 5).

1 teacher = 1 teacher's salary
1 intern = ⅔ of a teacher's salary
1 teaching assistant = ½ of a teacher's salary
1 clerk = ⅖ of a teacher's salary

Local conditions will govern these ratios. No matter what they are, the ratio between prevailing salaries of different categories of staff must be considered before final decisions can be made on staff utilization.

The Concept of Staff Factor Ratio   It is necessary to relate the total staff factors (F) to the definition of a full instructional load given above. For any row of Figure 10.1, once the total staff factors have been determined, administration asks, "How much of the total defined load of this kind of staff is represented by this total

FIGURE 10.1. COMPUTING STAFF REQUIREMENTS—ENGLISH DEPARTMENT

	Category of staff		Total staff modules	Instruction weight ratio	Total staff factors	Staff factor ratio	Teacher equivalents	
							Instruction	Support
LARGE GROUP	Instruction	T	10	2.0	20	0.020	0.40	XX
		I	1	2.0	2	0.012	0.02	XX
		TA	11	2.0	22	0.008	0.17	XX
	Support	TA	20	XX	20	0.008	XX	0.16
		C	40	XX	40	0.005	XX	0.20
LABORATORY	Instruction	T	45	1.0	45	0.020	0.90	XX
		I	73	1.0	73	0.012	0.87	XX
		TA	93	1.0	97	0.008	0.77	XX
	Support	TA	140	XX	140	0.008	XX	1.12
		C	40	XX	40	0.005	XX	0.02

SMALL GROUP	Instruction	T	260	1.5	390	0.020	7.80	XX
		I	26	1.5	39	0.012	0.46	XX
		TA	0	1.5	0	0.008	0	XX
	Support	TA	220	XX	220	0.008	XX	1.76
		C	40	XX	40	0.005	XX	0.20

Totals   11.39   3.64

Grand total   15.03

Note: 3.64/15.03 = 24 per cent of total teacher equivalents is noncertified staff support—to be devoted to relieving the professional teacher of many necessary duties which do not require professional training.

169

of staff factors?" A staff factor ratio becomes necessary. This is determined as follows:

$$\text{SFR} = \begin{matrix} \text{staff factor ratio} \\ \text{for any kind of} \\ \text{instructional or} \\ \text{support staff} \end{matrix} = \frac{1}{\begin{matrix} \text{number of staff-load} \\ \text{modules representing} \\ \text{a full instructional or} \\ \text{support load for this} \\ \text{category of staff} \end{matrix}} \times \begin{matrix} \text{teacher} \\ \text{equivalent} \\ \text{for this} \\ \text{staff} \\ \text{category} \end{matrix}$$

From the definitions previously given:

$$\text{SFR for teacher} = \frac{1}{50} \times 1 = 0.020$$

$$\text{SFR for intern} = \frac{1}{54} \times \frac{2}{3} = 0.012$$

$$\text{SFR for teacher aid} = \frac{1}{60} \times \frac{1}{2} = 0.008$$

$$\text{SFR for clerk} = \frac{1}{80} \times \frac{2}{5} = 0.005$$

It must be emphasized that the ratios derived here are not to be regarded as optimal for any or all contexts. They illustrate an approach to a problem that must be solved in each school. Within this limitation the process is recommended as valid.

The column headed "Staff factor ratio" in Figure 10.1 illustrates how each ratio is associated with an appropriate staff category and method of instruction for an English department.

The Concept of Teacher Equivalents   The administration can now answer the questions posed in the previous paragraphs. The total staff factors for each category of staff assigned to each kind of instruction within a department are converted into "teacher equivalents" (see the final columns of Figure 10.1).

The teacher equivalent = (total staff factors)(staff factor ratio)

By summing the teacher equivalents in each of the last two rows of Figure 10.1 and multiplying these sums by the prevailing average teacher's salary in the district, the cost of instruction and instructional support for the English department of the school is obtained. Necessarily this information becomes vital in making budget decisions. Once such decisions are made, the resulting ratio,

$$\frac{\text{Total pupils enrolled in English}}{\text{Teacher equivalents in English}} = \text{pupil-teacher ratio}$$

sets the upper limits within which departmental leadership must confine its staffing plans. A great increase in flexibility, available to departments as they adjust staff decisions to budget requirements, predictably will be realized by operation of the new design.

The fact that for some teachers other variables (e.g., part-time assignment to supervisory or administrative duties) must be considered in making load appraisals in no way invalidates the above approach. Job analyses can identify these other load factors which can be incorporated in the overall calculations. One possible approach to this would establish additional categories of staff instructional support, providing for professional support staff in addition to clerks and teacher aids. In this way deans, department heads, vice principals, counselors, psychologists, etc., can be integrated into the overall determinations of staff utilization. The primary concern here has been confined to instructional staff, however.

The example for English in Figure 10.1 typifies the process of computing staff requirements for all areas of knowledge.

Weekly Schedules for Teachers

Implementation of innovations proposed by the new design will change customary daily schedules, traditionally repeated each day, for the semester or the year. The possible patterns become numerous. It will suffice to examine three of these which are illustrated in Figures 10.2*a*, *b*, and *c*. Note there are 16 time modules in the day, totaling 80 periods of responsibility for the five-day schedule cycle.

The English teacher whose program is shown in Figure 10.2*a* has these responsibilities:

1. *Participation in general or special faculty meetings.* Five periods are kept open for this, totaling 2½ hours per week and located in period 1 each day. This does not mean a faculty meeting every morning of the week. It does make possible such meetings at this time, when appropriate.

2. *Departmental meetings.* Five periods weekly, or 2½ hours, are reserved for these, one hour (periods 15 and 16) on Monday and Wednesday, one-half hour (period 16) on Friday (perhaps not an appropriate time). This together with (1) above allocates 10 periods of the 80 available for necessary communication and planning with other faculty members.

3. *Guidance instruction.* Five periods, 2½ hours per week, are reserved for this important responsibility, to be used as described in Chapter 7. This teacher meets with his guidance group on Monday, Wednesday, and Friday for one-half hour. On Tuesday and Thursday he has one-half hour for individual counseling with students, for meetings with the grade-level counselor, or with parents.

4. *Large-group instruction.* This teacher has two half-hour lectures to give—on Tuesday morning, third period, and on Thursday morning, seventh period. Here he meets with all students assigned to group III of the eighth grade. Referring back to Figure 9.5, this might include as many as 120 students.

5. *Small-group instruction.* On Monday this teacher meets for one hour with four small groups of about 20 students each. Three of these sections include students from group III of the eighth grade. The fourth section is a phase of group IV English

FIGURE 10.2*a*. ILLUSTRATING AN ENGLISH TEACHER'S WEEKLY SCHEDULE

Per.	M	T	W	Th	F
1	FM	FM	FM	FM	FM
2	G	G(IS)	G	G(IS)	G
3	⌐ SG IV 7	LG III 8	xx	⌐ SG III 8	xx
4	⌊ SG IV 7	SG IV 10	xx	⌊ SG III 8	xx
5	⌐ SG III 8	xx	xx	⌐ SG III 8	xx
6	⌊ SG III 8	xx	⌐ SG IV 7	⌊ SG III 8	xx
7	⌐ SG III 8	xx	⌊ SG IV 7	LG III 8	xx
8	⌊ SG III 8	Lunch	Lunch	Lunch	Lunch
9	Lunch	xx	xx	⌐ SG III 8	xx
10	⌐ SG III 8	⌐ SG III 8	⌐ Lab III 8	⌊ SG III 8	xx
11	⌊ SG III 8	⌊ SG III 8	⌊ Lab III 8	⌐ SG III 8	xx
12	xx	⌐ SG III 8	⌐ Lab III 8	⌊ SG III 8	xx
13	⌐ Lab III 8	⌊ SG III	⌊ Lab III 8	⌐ SG III 8	xx
14	⌊ Lab III 8	⌐ SG III 8	xx	⌊ SG III 8	xx
15	DM	⌊ SG III 8	DM	⌐ SG III 8	xx
16	DM	xx	DM	⌊ SG III 8	xx

Code:
FM . . . .   faculty meetings as needed
SG IV 7 or SG III 8. . . .   small group, kind of group, and grade level
LG III 8 . . . .   large group, kind of group, and grade level
[. . . . .   number of periods in one section
G . . . .   group guidance
G(IS) . . . .   individual guidance
Lab III 8 . . . .   laboratory, kind of group, and grade level
DM . . . .   departmental meetings
xx . . . .   unscheduled

FIGURE 10.2b. SHOWING AN INTERN'S SCHEDULE IN THE
ENGLISH DEPARTMENT—LIGHT LOAD

Per.	M	T	W	Th	F
1	FM	FM	FM	FM	FM
2	xx	xx	xx	xx	xx
3	┌ Lab V 8	┌ SG II 9	┌SG II 9	┌ Lab II 11	┌ Lab I 10
4	└ Lab V 8	└ SG II 9	└SG II 9	Lab II 11	└ Lab I 10
5	┌ Lab V 8	xx	┌Lab IV 12	Lab II 11	┌ Lab I 9
6	└ Lab V 8	xx	└Lab IV 12	└ Lab II 11	└ Lab I 9
7	┌ Lab I 10	┌ Lab V 12	xx	SG II 9	xx
8	└ Lab I 10	└ Lab V 12	xx	xx	xx
9	Lunch	Lunch	Lunch	Lunch	Lunch
10	xx	┌ SG II 9	xx	xx	xx
11	xx	└ SG II 9	xx	xx	xx
12	xx	xx	xx	┌ SG II 9	┌ Lab II 10
13	xx	xx	xx	└ SG II 9	Lab II 10
14	xx	xx	xx	xx	└ Lab II 10
15	DM	xx	DM	xx	xx
16	DM	xx	DM	xx	DM

Code:
FM . . . . faculty meetings as needed
SG IV 7 or SG III 8 . . . . small group, kind of group, and grade level
LG III 8 . . . . large group, kind of group, and grade level
[. . . . . number of periods in one section
G . . . . group guidance
G(IS) . . . . individual guidance
Lab III 8 . . . . laboratory, kind of group, and grade level
DM . . . . departmental meetings
xx . . . . unscheduled

FIGURE 10.2c. SHOWING AN INTERN'S SCHEDULE IN THE
ENGLISH DEPARTMENT—HEAVIER LOAD ASSIGNMENT

Per.	M	T	W	Th	F
1	FM	FM	FM	FM	FM
2	xx	xx	xx	xx	xx
3	⌐ Lab V 8	⌐ SG II 9	⌐SG II 9	⌐Lab II 11	⌐Lab I 10
4	⌐ Lab V 8	⌐ SG II 9	⌐SG II 9	Lab II 11	⌐ Lab I 10
5	⌐ Lab V 8	xx	⌐Lab IV 12	Lab II 11	⌐Lab I 9
6	⌐Lab V 8	xx	⌐Lab IV 12	⌐Lab II 11	⌐ Lab I 9
7	⌐ Lab I 10	⌐ Lab V 12	xx	SG II 9	xx
8	⌐ Lab I 10	⌐ Lab V 12	xx	Lunch	Lunch
9	Lunch	Lunch	Lunch	⌐Lab III 11	⌐ Lab I 9
10	⌐ Lab I 9	⌐ SG II 9	⌐Lab I 10	Lab III 11	⌐ Lab I 9
11	⌐ Lab I 9	⌐ SG II 9	⌐Lab I 10	⌐Lab III 11	xx
12	⌐ Lab I 9	xx	⌐Lab III 11	⌐SG II 9	⌐ Lab II 10
13	⌐ Lab I 9	SG II 9	Lab III 11	⌐SG II 9	Lab II 10
14	xx	⌐ Lab V 12	⌐Lab III 11	xx	⌐Lab II 10
15	DM	⌐ Lab V 12	DM	⌐Lab I 10	xx
16	DM	xx	DM	⌐Lab I 10	DM

from grade 7. On Tuesday the teacher leads one small-group section one-half hour in length, for group IV students of grade 10, and
three one-hour sections with grade 8, group III students. On
Wednesday he meets again with a grade 7, group IV section for
one hour. On Thursday he leads six small-group sections of one hour
each with the same eighth-grade group III students he met on

Monday and Tuesday. During the week his assignment for small-group leadership thus includes:

	Total periods
One half-hour phase with tenth grade, group IV	1
Two one-hour phases with seventh grade, group IV	4
Twelve one-hour phases with eighth grade, group III	24
Total assignment to small groups	29

6. *Laboratory instruction.* On Monday the teacher has a one-hour laboratory assignment, meeting during periods 13 and 14 with a laboratory section of grade 8, group III students. On Wednesday he is scheduled to meet with two laboratory sections of one hour each from the same eighth-grade group (periods 10 through 13). His total laboratory time for the week—6 periods.

7. *Time for lunch.* The schedule provides one-half hour each day, either eighth or ninth period, for lunch.

8. *Time for planning, evaluation, individual work with students, faculty, or support staff.* There remains from the total 80 periods of weekly responsibility, 23 unscheduled periods. The teacher has complete freedom to determine how he will best utilize this time. The time is not distributed evenly over the days of the week.

Weekly Distribution of Unscheduled Time

	Periods
Monday	1
Tuesday	5
Wednesday	5
Thursday	0
Friday	12
Total	23

9. Summary of the English teacher's schedule shown in Figure 10.2a.

Periods for faculty and departmental meetings.................. 10
Periods for lunch... 5
Periods for instructional leadership:
Guidance.................... 5
Large group................ 2
Small group................ 29
Laboratory 6
Total 42
Unscheduled time 23
Total 80

The sample schedule just described is not offered as an ideal one. It can be criticized on several counts, perhaps the more important being these:

1. The overall load is a bit heavy. Applying the instruction weight ratio to his instructional load gives:

2 periods large group × 2   = 4
29 periods small group × 1.5 = 43.5
6 laboratory periods × 1.0 = 6
Total staff factors   53.5

More important, the number of distinctly different groups to prepare for weekly totals *seven,* counting the guidance group. This should be reduced, and perhaps support staff can help in doing so. There is an advantage in giving this teacher experience with grade 7, 8, and 10 groups during the same semester; i.e., it promotes better curriculum sequence and team planning. However, it costs in added preparations.

2. The small-group load on Thursday is too high. Starting with period 3, this teacher is committed to six hours of small-group discussions plus a half-hour large-group lecture. Preferably there ought to be at least a one-period break, besides the half-hour lunch. On Friday this teacher, after his guidance meeting, has a relatively free day. One can anticipate his saying, "Friday, thank

heavens!" Some teachers will respond well to the heavy Thursday load, others not.

Certainly, if building facilities are adequate to provide this teacher a study and work area to be used while not engaged in the act of instruction, the sample schedule has advantages over the traditional one. Traditionally, over one week of 5 eight-hour days, the English teacher devotes fifty periods to instruction, ten each day. He has one-half hour before classes start in the morning and one-half hour after school, plus two periods during the day for planning, staff meetings, and evaluation, totaling 20 periods per week. The sample schedule given here includes 33 periods for these purposes, in the same total time block. Aside from additional time, the new schedule incorporates staff support to permit the English teacher to use his time for professional rather than for routine responsibilities.

Figures 10.2*b* and *c* illustrate possible weekly schedules for an English department intern or beginning teacher. The first schedule typifies a light load (approximately half that of a regular teacher) which might be appropriate when integrated with a teacher-training program of a nearby university or college. The intern's assignment is summarized as follows:

Periods weekly

Faculty and departmental meetings..................	10
Small-group leadership............................	9
Laboratory leadership............................	21
Lunch..	5
Time for observation, planning, unscheduled staff support.................................	35
	80

This intern does not have guidance responsibilities. He has ample time to observe experienced teachers in all phases of their practice during the week. Converting his assignment to teacher equivalents gives for instruction:

$$\text{Small group: } 9 \times 1.5 = 13.5$$
$$\text{Laboratory: } 21 \times 1.0 = \underline{21.0}$$
$$34.5$$

$$34.5 \times 0.012 = 0.414$$

He should be paid about half the beginning teacher's salary. Figure 10.2c illustrates a possible weekly schedule for an intern which represents more closely a full load in terms of teacher equivalents. Summarizing this:

	Periods weekly
Faculty and departmental meetings.................	10
Small-group instructional leadership................	10
Laboratory leadership............................	39
Lunch..	5
Unscheduled time...............................	16
Total.......................................	80

Determining the teacher equivalents of the above load:

$$\text{Small group: } 10 \times 1.5 = 15$$
$$\text{Laboratory: } 39 \times 1.0 = \underline{39}$$
$$54$$

$$54 \times 0.012 = 0.648 \text{ teacher equivalents}$$

A fair compensation for this intern assignment would thus be about two-thirds the salary of a beginning teacher in this department.

Weekly Schedules for Students

Traditionally the high school student followed a daily schedule, repeated five times a week, for the semester or the school year. Schedules followed by students in schools which have adapted innovations of the new design will repeat weekly, rather than daily, and have many interesting variations. Examples of three such schedules are illustrated in Figures 10.3a, b, and c.

FIGURE 10.3*a*. A SAMPLE SCHEDULE FOR STUDENT ROBERT, GRADE 7

Per.	M	T	W	Th	F
1	IS, T, or A	IS, T, or A	IS, T, or A	IS, T, or A	IS, T, or A
2	G(LG)	G(IS)	G(LG)	G(IS)	G(LG)
3	Sci. LG IV	Eng. LG III	Sci. LG II	Sci. lab IV	Eng. LG IV
4	SS SG I	FL lab III	FL lab III	Sci. lab IV	FL lab III
5	SS SG I	Arts LG I	Arts LG I	Sci. lab IV	IS
6	Eng. lab III	Eng. lab III	Arts LG I	SS LG I	Eng. lab III
7	Eng. lab III	Eng. lab III	Arts LG I	IS	Eng. lab III
8	Math LG IV	Math LG IV	Lunch	Math LG IV	Math LG IV
9	PE LG II	Lunch	Math LG IV	Math lab IV	SS LG I
10	Lunch	SS LG I	Math lab IV	Lunch	Lunch
11	FL lab III	IS	Eng. SG III	FL SG III	Sci. SG IV
12	IS	IS	Eng. SG III	FL SG III	Sci. SG IV
13	IS	IS	IS	Eng. SG III	Math lab IV
14	Arts LG I	IS	PE lab II	Eng. SG III	PE lab II
15	Arts LG I	PE lab II	PE lab II	Arts LG I	PE lab II
16	Arts LG I	PE lab II	IS	PE LG II	IS

T = Transportation to school
A = Activities
IS = Individual study

FIGURE 10.3*b*. A SAMPLE SCHEDULE FOR STUDENT CHARLES, GRADE 10

Per.	M	T	W	Th	F
1	IS, T, or A	IS, T, or A	IS, T, or A	IS, T, or A	IS, T, or A
2	G(LG)	G(IS)	G(LG)	G(IS)	G(LG)
3	FL lab IV	IS	FL lab IV	PE LG IV	FL lab IV
4	FL SG II	IS	SS LG IV	IS	SS LG IV
5	Sci. LG III	Sci. lab III	Sci. LG III	Sci. SG III	Sci. SG III
6	PE lab IV	Sci. lab III	PE LG IV	Sci. SG III	PE lab IV
7	PE lab IV	PE LG IV	PE LG IV	PE SG IV	PE lab IV
8	IS	IS	IS	IS	IS
9	Lunch	Lunch	Lunch	Lunch	Lunch
10	Math LG I	Math lab I	Math LG I	Math lab I	Math LG I
11	Eng. lab III	FL lab IV	Eng. SG III	FL lab IV	FL SG IV
12	Eng. lab III	Eng. LG III	IS	Eng. lab III	FL SG IV
13	Arts LG III	SS SG IV	SS lab IV	Eng. lab III	IS
14	Arts LG III	SS SG IV	SS lab IV	SS SG IV	Arts LG III
15	Arts LG III	SS SG IV	SS lab IV	SS SG IV	Arts LG III
16	SS SG IV	IS	SS lab IV	SS SG IV	Arts LG III

FIGURE 10.3c. SHOWING ELEVENTH-GRADE STUDENT TOM, WHO IS PARTICIPATING
IN A SCHOOL-SPONSORED WORK-EXPERIENCE PROGRAM

Per.	M	T	W	Th	F
1	IS, T, or A	IS, T, or A	IS, T, or A	IS, T, or A	IS, T, or A
2	G(SG)	G(IS)	G(SG)	G(IS)	G(SG)
3	Sci. SG IV	Arts LG IV	Math lab IV	Arts LG IV	Arts SG IV
4	Sci. SG IV	Arts LG IV	Math lab IV	Arts LG IV	Arts SG IV
5	FL lab I	Arts LG IV	FL lab I	Arts LG IV	Arts SG IV
6	Eng. SG IV	Eng. lab IV	Sci. lab I	Eng. lab IV	Eng. SG IV
7	Eng. SG IV	Eng. lab IV	Sci. lab I	FL SG I	Eng. SG IV
8	Lunch	SS SG I	Lunch	Lunch	Math lab IV
9	SS LG I	Lunch	SS LG I	Eng. lab IV	Lunch
10	PE lab II	Eng. lab IV	PE lab II	SS lab I	Sci. LG I
11	PE lab II	PE LG II	PE lab II	SS lab I	PE lab II
12					
13			Periods 12–16 are scheduled for		
14			participation in a school-sponsored		
15			work-experience program.		
16					

T = Transportation to school
A = Activities
IS = Individual study

Seventh grader Robert distributes his weekly time as follows (see Figure 10.3*a*):

No. of periods

Science: Two LG sessions, M, W, one lab section, Th, one SG section, F. .	7
Social studies: Two SG sections, M, Th, two LG sessions, T, F.......	5
English: Three lab sections, M, T, F, two LG sessions, T, F, two SG sections, W, Th...	12
Mathematics: Five LG sessions, M, T, W, Th, F, three lab sections, W, Th, F..	8
Foreign language: Four lab sections, M, T, W, F, one SG section, Th. .	6
Art: Four LG sessions, M, T, W, Th............................	8
Phys. ed.: Two LG sessions, M, Th, three lab sections, T, W, F.......	8
Individual study (depending on 1st-period decision).................	11 to 16
Lunch..	5
Guidance: Three SG sections, two IS............................	5
Total..	80

Note that Robert is in:

> group I for social studies, art
> group II for physical education
> group III for English, foreign language
> group IV for science, mathematics

He may commit the first period to either school activities, individual study, or travel to school. He has in addition 11 periods a week for individual study and concentration.

Tenth grader Charles distributes his weekly time as follows (see Figure 10.3*b*):

Periods

Foreign languages: Five lab sections, M, T, W, Th, F, two SG sections, M, F	8
Science: Two LG sessions, M, W, one lab section, T, two SG sections, Th, F	7
Physical education: Two LG sessions, T, Th, one SG section, Th, three lab sections, M, W, F..	9
Social studies: Three LG sessions, M, W, F, two SG sections, T, Th, one lab section, W..	13
Individual study (depending on use of period 1).....................	11 to 16
Mathematics: Three LG sessions, M, W, F, two lab sections, T, Th......	5
English: One LG session, T, two lab sections, M, Th, one SG section, W. .	6
Arts: Two LG sessions, M, F...................................	6
Lunch..	5
Guidance: Two IS, T, Th, three LG sessions, M, W, F.................	5
Total..	80

Note that tenth grader Charles is in:

group III for science, English, arts
group IV for foreign languages, physical education, social studies
group I for mathematics

He has from 11 to 16 periods for individual study, activities, and concentration.

Eleventh grader Tom (see Figure 10.3c) includes in his weekly schedule 25 periods for a school-sponsored work-experience program. His remaining 55 periods are scheduled as follows:

Periods

Science: Two SG sections, M, F, one lab section, W	5
Foreign languages: Two lab sections, M, W, one SG section, Th	3
English: Two SG sections, M, F, four lab sections, two on T, two on Th	9
Mathematics: Two lab sections, W, F	3
Social studies: Two LG sessions, M, W, one SG section, T, one lab section, Th	5
Physical education: Two LG sessions, T, F, two lab sections, M, W	6
Arts: Two LG sessions, T, Th, one SG section, F	9
Lunch	5
Guidance	5
Activities or individual study	5
Total	55

Note that Tom is in:

group I for foreign languages, social studies
group II for physical education
group IV for science, English, mathematics, arts

The reader should again be reminded that the above modules, time and staff allotments, course designations, instructional staff weight ratios, and teacher and pupil schedules represent only examples of alternatives. The authors have little doubt that once the conventional barriers are down, enthusiastic and imaginative curriculum designers will apply those features which suit their unique purposes.

A CONCLUDING NOTE

To sum up, what does *A New Design for High School Education: Assuming a Flexible Schedule* mean?

Our statement challenges the educational program in high schools today which is based upon outdated assumptions about the use of time. The school schedule is singled out for attention because it is the scheme by which time is distributed to the various parts of the school program, and it has proved to be a powerful weapon, for good or ill, in the realization of new curricular developments. Unfortunately, tradition too often decrees the schedule. "It can't be scheduled" has become the knell of innumerable new ideas.

When the curriculum proposals for *A New Design for High School Education* began to founder upon the question "Can it be scheduled?" the investigation took a dramatic new turn. By using modern technology, we asked, could a general scheme for scheduling be worked out that would encourage, not block, experimentation? The model presented in Chapter 3 was the first major result of this inquiry. Three years of additional work produced a computer technology to implement this model. Professor Oakford's contribution in the development of the computer-based Stanford School Scheduling System may well be one of the more important contemporary technological contributions to the educational programs of the high school.

Schools that have begun to implement the ideas set forth in the new design and that are using computers to generate their schedules have also begun to adopt a variety of educational practices which they had not previously considered. New curricular alternatives have become possible, causing a definite break with traditional organization and teaching. One need only walk into one of these schools to observe that something different is happening. Here are the fruits of technology being harvested. The general academic pace has been quickened. Teachers have more time for teaching. Pupils have more time for learning. In each of the schools 30 per cent of their students' time has been programmed for independent and individual study. Libraries are full of students. Circulation of books, especially nonfiction, is sharply up. Discipline problems are down. Class size varies from 5 to 350. Period length varies from fifteen minutes to almost three hours. The individualization of instruction is different in these schools. Achievement rather than time spent in a class becomes the criterion for successful completion of a course in these schools.

The development of independent study programs where students are provided with an opportunity to budget their time independently have burgeoned. Resource centers, as illustrated in the discussion of the mathematics laboratory in Chapter 3, have developed in the schools as an exciting location for independent work. Homework may wither as the resource centers flourish.

Knowledge of the process of learning can be applied in these schools. Spaced and massed distribution of practice can be employed as appropriate. Flexible schools are using programmed learning as better materials become available. Flexible schedules permit nongraded programs, where age no longer is the predominate factor in grouping. These schools can systematically investigate new ways to employ professional personnel in team combinations with various levels of assistants.

A variety of major curricular reforms has been proposed and tried during the past decade. These reforms have been directed for the most part at the improvement of specific subjects. Large public and private expenditures have gone into these efforts. Increasingly schools are having difficulty in adjusting their programs to meet competing demands upon time, staff, and facilities. There is need for coordination and for trying new concepts of school organization if these many promising separate programs are to realize their full potential for upholding the quality of education in the schools.

As these innovations are evaluated and revised, freedom from schedule limitations may open even greater new possibilities. The urgent question now is: How can schools reorganize their programs to take advantage of the new mathematics, the new science, and the new language teaching, and still ensure adequate attention to the humanities, the applied arts, and other essentials of a liberal education? Is there a more adequate framework within which the total high school program can be cast so that it can make use of the many technological innovations available?

What is to be concluded? To return to the beginning, remember that *A New Design for High School Education* has been proposed to meet the central educational challenge of these times: ensuring the essential education for all young citizens, and at the same time enabling each one to develop his unique talents to the maximum. The accomplishment of this high purpose is more than has ever been required of schools in the past.

The frightening capacity of man's reach for knowledge and power has become sobering indeed in recent times. Can a school—the high school in particular—make a difference? Can secondary education be so managed as to help ensure a constructive rather than a disastrous result from the application of human intelligence to the physical and social affairs of mankind?

Considering the wide range of human abilities and the circumstances which individuals must face, the necessity for a flexible rather than a rigid approach to the conduct of education becomes readily apparent.

INDEX

189